Online Learning Strategies

Association Models for Success

Don Dea and Hugh K. Lee

A Grant Project Funded by the Foundation of the
American Society of Association Executives

American Society of Association Executives
Washington, D.C.

Information in this book is accurate as of the time of publication and consistent with standards of good practice in the general management community. As research and practice advance, however, standards may change. For this reason, it is recommended that readers evaluate the applicability of any recommendation in light of particular situations and changing standards.

American Society of Association Executives
1575 I Street, NW
Washington, DC 20005
Phone: (202) 626-2723
Fax: (202) 408-9634
E-mail: books@asaenet.org

George Moffat, Publisher
Linda Munday, Director of Book Publishing
Anna Nunan, Book Acquisitions Coordinator
Zachary Dorsey, Production Coordinator
Cover and interior design by Atelier Design, Inc.

This book is available at a special discount when ordered in bulk quantities. For information, contact the ASAE Member Service Center at (202) 371-0940.

A complete catalog of titles is available on the ASAE Web site at http://www.asaenet.org

Dea, Don.
    Online learning strategies : association models for success / Don Dea and Hugh K. Lee.
        p. cm.
    ISBN 0-88034-160-2
    1. Computer-assisted instruction—United States. 2. Internet (Computer network)
in education—United States. 3. Adult education—United States—Societies, etc.
    4. Professional associations—United States. I. Lee, Hugh K. II. American Society of
Association Executives. III. Title.
    LB1028.5.D34 1999   99-32095
    374.'13344—dc21   CIP

Printed in the United States of America.

10 9 8 7 6 5 4 3 2 1

Contents

Foreword

Trends, environmental scans, and electronic polling of audiences at American Society of Association Executives ASAE) general sessions indicate that members want to be educated and receive information online—when, where, and how they find it most convenient. Based on this quest for knowledge via online education coupled with the demand on association executives to find ways to better use technology to deliver programs and services, the ASAE Foundation saw the need to provide a leading-edge model on how to do just that in one of the primary areas owned by associations: education.

In 1997, the Foundation awarded a grant to Fusion Productions, Webster, New York, to research this area of interest, and one of the results of the research is this study. The Foundation initiated this research to help associations understand how other organizations are using online education, identify the different approaches to offering online education, and answer questions such as, What tools and processes are necessary for advanced online education? This research will arm associations with the information they need to take charge of their future as premier providers of education.

The research produced by Fusion Productions has advanced the mission of the Foundation to enhance the future effectiveness of the association community and to maximize that community's effect on society through education and research. This study provides the association profession a comprehensive review of where online education is today, a working model of where it will be in the near future, and both the tools and guidelines associations need to be at the forefront of this dramatic evolution.

Liz Jackson
President, Associated Luxury Hotels
Washington, D.C.
ASAE Foundation Chair (1998–99)

Acknowledgments

Gratefully acknowledged here are the special contributions of the entire Executive Panel: Marsha Rhea, CAE, executive vice president and chief operating officer, and Michelle Mason, manager, Research Programs, ASAE Foundation; industry advisers, including Phil Clark, president and CEO, IBT Group, Falls Church, Va.; Elliot Masie, president, the Masie Center, Saratoga Springs, N.Y.; Anne Blouin, CAE, director of education, American Society for Training and Development, Alexandria, Va.; Wayne Hodgins, board president, Computer Education Management Association, Los Gatos, Calif.; and Fusion Productions' staff members Stephen S. Nazarian, technical producer, for managing the project, and Suzanne Minemier, coordinator of office services, for research design and cross-tabulations.

Special thanks also go to the following individuals who shared their experiences and expertise on behalf of this study:

- Naresh Bala, vice president sales and marketing, Mentorware, Santa Clara, Calif.
- R. David Bender, executive director, Special Libraries Association, Washington, D.C.
- Caroline Cheung, product application manager, Avalon Information Technologies, Brampton, Ontario, Canada
- Britta Glade, vice president marketing, Allen Communication, Salt Lake City, Utah
- Tom Glaser, director of Instructional Resources, State University of New York, Morrisville, N.Y.
- Karen Hackett, chief operating officer, American College of Healthcare Executives, Chicago
- Terri Hedegaard, vice president for Distance Learning, University of Phoenix
- Jerry Horsewood, president, Avilar Technologies, Laurel, Md.
- Robin Kriegel, executive director, American Association of Medical Society Executives, Chicago
- Kathy McGuire, manager, Distance Learning Program, University of California at Los Angeles
- Paul Mooney, program manager, Hewlett Packard, Palo Alto, Calif.

- Ginger Nichols, president, GinnCommGroup, San Francisco
- Eva Perlman, NLTN manager, Association of Public Health Laboratories, Washington, D.C.
- Jean Rhame, professional affairs manager, the American Association for Clinical Chemistry, Inc., Washington, D.C.
- David Sachs, assistant dean, Computer Science Information Systems, PACE University, White Plains, N.Y.
- Eileen Tafte, director, dean of the Virtual Institute, Association of Public Safety Communications Officials International, South Daytona, Fla.
- Jon Walker, project manager, Dow Chemical, Midland, Mich.

Finally, we leave you with a thought that we feel best summarizes what online education should be striving for: The only sustainable competitive advantage is the ability to learn and apply the right stuff faster.

Hugh K. Lee
President
Fusion Productions

Don Dea
Co-Owner
Fusion Productions

Introduction

The opportunity is enormous. Our global economy is changing rapidly and is becoming increasingly knowledge based. These conditions have increased the demand for faster and better learning and training techniques that are available anywhere and anytime. If ever there was a golden age for associations, it is here and now. Association members and the organizations for which they work are demanding the best of what associations have to offer. They are searching for:

- The ability to collect solutions and targeted content customized to their profession/industry groups quickly and effectively;

- Proven training programs and qualified faculty; and

- Credible and safe communities in which to exchange ideas and learn from peers.

The question is, will associations seize the opportunity or leave the door open for other, more innovative competitors (whether profit or nonprofit) to leapfrog them on a critical need of their membership, and thus gain a significant advantage in the market?

A recent ASAE Foundation study shows that online education has begun to make an impact, with 10.6 percent of the study participants reporting that they use online education today. Compare that with the percentage of those who are using the more traditional training formats, such as computer-based training (11.7%) and video (17%), and the growth is impressive.

It is likely that Web training will continue to grow at a greater rate compared with traditional options. The survey results show more than 17 percent of associations were planning to offer online education for the first time by the end of 1998, with 30 percent undecided. The findings are consistent with information presented in the 1998 American Society for Training and Development's State of the Industry Report, which found that 21 percent of leading corporations are delivering training via learning technologies. According to the report, "companies that engage in more competency-based training, high-performance work practices, and innovative training practices are more likely to use learning technologies. Such results support the idea that innovative companies are moving toward learning technologies and away from classroom instruction." The opportunity and consequences for associations can be enormous.

What are the challenges facing innovative associations that wish to move toward a portfolio of services that includes online education? Interviews with over 200 associations indicate that a major barrier to online education is a lack of knowledge on how to deliver truly interactive education online. In most cases, associations are not taking advantage of their Web site's capability to get closer to their members because they do not know how to do so. Key areas of concern for associations today include software tools needed to employ online education, the platform to use, design considerations, existing comparative models that can be quickly adapted, and future considerations.

The ASAE Foundation study on online education and associations reveals that the issue of online education also raises traditional challenges, such as reinforcing the fundamentals of instructional design. Respondents rated basic techniques and tools highest in terms of importance to online education. On a scale of one to five, with one being least important, each of the following techniques was rated most important:

- learning objectives (51%)
- hands-on exercises (49%)
- online support resources (links) (40%)
- online self-assessment tools (38%)

From a technical perspective, those elements rated highest include:

- online help (54%)
- help via e-mail response in 24 hours (53%)
- discussion forums (31%)
- instructor-led chat sessions (21%)
- synchronous audio and presentation (20%)

Other survey highlights include:

- Almost 53 percent of respondents are interested in creating courses for online delivery.
- Quality of learning and cost are the most important issues when considering the deployment of online education.
- Sixty-seven percent felt that computer-based education and Web-based online education are cost efficient for the association.

- Fifty-two percent strongly or somewhat agree that classroom-based material needs to be significantly redesigned for the Web.

Fifty-seven percent of respondents strongly or somewhat agree that online education should be available to both members and nonmembers.

A large majority of respondents create their own customized education (78.8%), and 65.2 percent of respondents use volunteer faculty to help develop their educational programs. Based on that information, the study focused on information and tools that would help associations and volunteer professionals build their online programs with customized packages rather than "off the shelf" packages.

Environmental scans also were conducted as part of the Foundation research project. From the scans, it became clear that online education is just beginning to emerge as a powerful standalone tool to enhance knowledge sharing or as an additional tool that is in many respects faster, better, and cheaper than traditional models of training. The allure of providing training anytime, anywhere, in multiple formats, and without the cost of travel and time away is great. Even the prestigious Harvard University has recently decided to provide educational programming online.

Although associations are not far behind the corporate and university worlds in their use of online education, the use of online education by leading corporations is growing at an impressive rate. Leading-edge corporations are having so much success with their online training programs that they are considering marketing these programs to other organizations, thereby becoming formidable competitors to associations for training dollars.

Associations are turning to online education for many reasons, including productivity, membership retention and acquisition, and competition. There is a series of fundamentals associations should consider to help them understand and move forward to establish online education capabilities. These fundamentals include:

- A business plan that provides a framework and vision for education
- A complete needs analysis of the target audience
- An effective program and platform design
- A coordinated development phase
- A proper evaluation of each program component
- An integrated management process

Once the fundamentals are reviewed, additional tactical considerations must be considered, such as:

- Instructors must become familiar with needed tools and how to deliver and support interactive and multimedia instruction on the Internet.

- Students must be trained in the use of the selected tools.

- Instructional methods must consider browser and bandwidth limitations.

- Performance of sound, video, and larger graphics must be considered with respect to available bandwidth.

- A trained staff is needed to handle server administration, access, and billing.

- Links to outside sources used in the program must be reviewed frequently because they are constantly changing.

- The program design must focus first on the student and learning environment, then on the technology.

The Foundation study shows that the gap between the winners and losers in online education is growing. Those who decided to make the jump to online education a year ago, despite existing problems (such as lack of software, lack of bandwidth, and an audience who behaviorally felt more comfortable in a classroom) have gained a significant jump on the competition. Over the past year or so, improved software has been released that allows online programs to be designed more quickly than before. In this same time period, new processes for converting content from traditional media to the Web have been created. Faculty who have experience in teaching and designing curricula for the Web together with their audiences are moving beyond the behavioral and cultural challenges of using the Web versus being taught in a classroom.

It all starts with a business plan and a strategy. An online education strategy increases the chances of success, ensures links to other activities, and reduces FUD (fear, uncertainty, and doubt).

Where do these advancements over the past year lead associations? Associations now can see the tip of the iceberg thanks to others who have explored the frontiers of online education before them. The Foundation's research and experience shows that online education will be an integral key to helping an organization build or improve its brand. A brand is much more than a symbol, name, or slogan. It is a "contract" of trust between an organization and its constituencies.

Developing a strong brand identity creates an asset that provides a distinct competitive advantage and value for an association.

To help build brand equity and capture many more of the benefits of providing online education, one should heed the advice of an executive from the Best Practices study featured in chapter 4: "Take a chance with online education—this is the future. Lead, don't follow." You may also want to apply the philosophies behind these other quotes:

> "We don't need to think more; we need to think differently."
> —Albert Einstein

> "Incrementalism is innovation's worst enemy."
> —Nicholas Negroponte

This report does not only state the results of the ASAE Foundation study on online education, but rather, it is designed to help those who were not on the cutting edge a year ago to catch up quickly. It is important to recognize that each individual association is unique in terms of experience, internal instructional design, programming capability, and type of educational content to be delivered. Therefore, readers may find one section more pertinent than another. For example:

- If an association internally has strong Web and instructional design experience, it may find the section describing courseware vendors (the Resource Directory) most valuable.

- If you have an elementary online model but are thinking about moving to a more dynamic and interactive program, the association online course should be your starting point (chapter 5).

- Associations trying to assess whether they should be in the business of online education may want to first review the scans, best practice tips, and case studies to see if they are ready for such an endeavor (chapters 2, 3, and 4).

Like anything else in the world of the Internet, this guide is only a snapshot in time. New technologies, new software, and new business models are constantly surfacing and evolving. One thing is for sure: the adaptation curve for online education is extremely fast, and you can use this manual to help you assess how your association can deploy online education to stay ahead of that curve.

1. What Is Online Education?

There is no simple definition of online education. However, for purposes of this study, the following definition is provided:

> Online education is instruction that is delivered through the Internet or an intranet, providing a visual environment, interactive experience, and customized learning process. The Internet consists primarily of the World Wide Web and e-mail using standard protocols, such as HTTP and FTP.

Distinctions

When you look at the terminology used to describe many new online concepts, it is quickly apparent that the people who create and name these new concepts try to relate them to familiar or traditional terms. Unfortunately, these terms have been evolving, and this has led to considerable confusion. (For definitions of terms used in this report, refer to the Glossary.) A good example of this is the interchangeable use of "education" and "training" with their Internet terms being "online education" and "Web-based training." Although these terms are closely related, they are not the same in a traditional environment or on the Internet.

The term "education" may be viewed as a spectrum of learning, from a traditional paper-based format to learning delivered with the help of technologies such as CD-ROM and the Internet. Therefore, "online education" would be learning delivered in the Internet part of the spectrum, by various methods (self-paced and live), using various protocols and applications.

"Training" refers to specific instruction designed to improve skills, change attitudes, or enhance knowledge. Web-based training applies to any kind of instructional material delivered via the Internet using enabling technologies, such as graphics, audio, video, etc.

Market Overview

To better understand online education, it is helpful to understand more about the market and where online education fits into the overall training spectrum. The total market for Web-based training is projected to grow from $200 million in 1997 to nearly $6 billion in 2002.

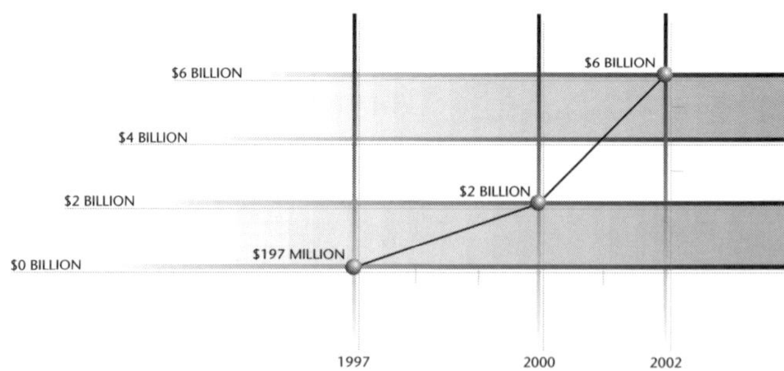

The online education market has experienced huge growth to this point, from nothing to over $200 million in the past few years. It is expected to reach $6 billion in the next few years. Combine this potential growth with the fact that larger corporations are devoting major resources to advancing online education and training, and it should be clear to associations that they need to understand what online education is.

Online Spectrum

The following spectrum of interactive learning represents where online education is in relation to other methods of delivering education. The spectrum ranges in delivery methods from asynchronous (self-paced, self-directed) to synchronous (live or "real time"). The focus of this study is online education.

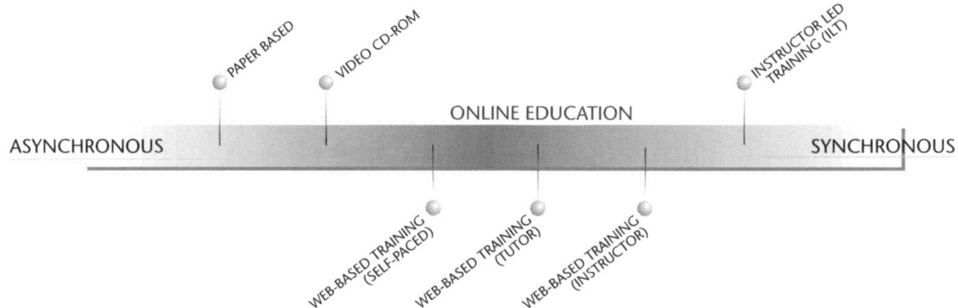

The following graphic shows a spectrum of delivery methods that focuses only on the online education area. It provides specific detail within the online segment, including investment scale, delivery requirements, and audience needs.

CATEGORY	ASYNCHRONOUS (SELF-PACED)	ASYNCHRONOUS (TUTOR)	SYNCHRONOUS (INSTRUCTOR)
INVESTMENT	SMALL	MEDIUM	LARGE
DELIVERY	REQUIRES BANDWIDTH	FLEXIBLE	REQUIRES BANDWIDTH
AUDIENCE	DESKTOP	MORE TECHNICAL	HIGHLY TECHNICAL

The ASAE Foundation World-Class Web Study conducted by Fusion Productions (1998) highlighted the rapid expansion of association "online presence" over the period 1995–97. During that period associations moved from 12 percent to over 78 percent having Web sites. The millennium promises the next wave of significant change for associations: the development and implementation of applications central to the purpose of associations. Associations will move from "being on the Web" to actually changing their core business models and servicing constituents in a fundamentally different manner.

Electronic commerce, community, and knowledge management directly affect the essence of an association's lifeline—education. With the growth of the Internet, and in particular the World Wide Web, the development of recent software, and increasing Internet speed, education now can be provided when, how, and where the market requires it. Education truly can become a tool for one-to-one marketing and personalization of association services.

The best way for an association to understand more about online education is to work this method of delivery into an association's education and training strategy. Key players with heavy influence are making increasing commitments to this delivery method, further proving its potential.

What is online education? It is a highly effective method of delivering education to members, providing associations with a powerful way to achieve member training and association goals.

The current environment of online education is heavily influenced by leading organizations, including universities, associations, corporations, and software vendors. Although both the methodology used by leaders to deliver instruction online and their target audience differ, the potential value from understanding the respective accomplishments of these leaders will benefit associations.

The study's review of the following organizations and their current position with online education revealed consistent themes. The first is that each group has a vested interest in helping its respective members, employees, and students gain knowledge. They have accepted this method of delivering instruction and are aggressively pursuing further advancements with executive support. The second is that they are not doing it alone. Recognizing the tremendous need for expertise in developing an online course with instruction, technology, management, industry knowledge, and more, these organizations tend to work with outside sources to develop their programs. The third and perhaps most important theme that runs through all sectors of the market is a shared understanding that delivering instruction online is much more than just an enhancement to traditional training methods.

Universities

The scan data for universities were collected from March 1, 1998, to July 15, 1998.

Associations and universities share a common goal of educating their target audience. A major difference between them is that universities have moved more quickly than associations to deliver their product, based on demand from an increasing number of working adults enrolled in college part time.

Many leading universities prefer to establish their online education programs by offering programs that are easily delivered online (i.e., software programs, mathematics, sciences, etc.); these typically use little interactivity. As courses and programs mature, institutions incorporate interactive elements into these basic courses. They then begin to present these online education programs as standard university courses, providing credit hours and applying the full administration process.

As part of the ASAE Foundation study on online education, a scan of university online education offerings was conducted. Several university programs were recommended by the project's executive panel and others involved in the study. From the recommendations, the University of Phoenix; the University of California, Los Angeles; and the State University of New York were selected for in-depth review.

University of Phoenix

The University of Phoenix (UOP) is the nation's largest private university; it has campuses in 65 cities. UOP began offering courses via the Internet in September 1989; it currently offers over 154 courses online. It offers bachelor's, master's, and doctoral degrees in business, management, technology, education, and nursing.

UOP's online format is similar to its campus-based educational model, which emphasizes group participation and the creation of learning communities. Using customized Internet software, students retrieve lectures, questions, and assignments from their instructor, then review them off-line. They participate in class discussions and study groups asynchronously via e-mail. They also have access to a full range of online research libraries and services. At the end of the week, students submit a summary of the concepts covered in class, and the instructor provides feedback on their progress via e-mail.

To ensure relevance, all UOP programs are continuously updated to reflect the latest industry concepts, methods, and practices. In addition, each faculty member is currently working in the fields he or she teaches. Courses are offered one at a time for six weeks, so students can explore each subject in more depth. Work experience can be converted to academic credit. Most students can earn their degree in about two years.

The cost of UOP education is average compared with other online universities and is based per credit hour. (Currently, online study group tuition is $375 per credit hour for undergraduate students and $470 per credit hour for graduate students.) Credit hours are assigned to a course based on the existing academic process in place at the university. Many financial aid options are available. More than 50 percent of UOP students receive tuition reimbursement from their employers.

All UOP students must have a high school diploma or equivalent, be at least 23 years old, be employed, and complete UOP's Comprehensive Cognitive Assessment.

UOP's vision for the future of online education includes increased collaboration between student and teacher, based on improvements in technology.

University of California, Los Angeles

The University of California, Los Angeles, (UCLA) began offering online learning in September 1996; more than 3,500 students from 49 states and 28 countries have participated to date in a UCLA Extension online course. UCLA Extension currently offers more than 100 online courses in business and management, education, computer programming, and writing.

All UCLA Extension online courses are taught using special software programs that facilitate the interaction between the online instructor and the students. The software tools used by UCLA are developed by Embanet, a company that specializes in providing asynchronous communications programs. Because each course is unique and taught by its own instructor, design and format varies much like in a traditional course experience. UCLA closely administers all issues related to academic design, management, instructional recruitment, and training.

Each course involves weekly or frequent assignments that must be completed. The flexibility provided by the asynchronous nature of the courses allows working individuals to complete weekly assignments around their own schedules and has contributed to an 85 percent course completion rate for online courses.

UCLA uses Online Learning.net to guide the marketing, promotion, and technical support of its online courses. Online Learning.net specializes in providing these support services to universities.

Course costs for a student range from $80 to $150 per quarter unit of academic credit. Units or credit hours are largely determined by the duration of the course. The average course costs between $400 and $500 as a whole.

UCLA's vision for the future is based on the belief that online courses and expanding technology will open new learning opportunities for working professionals, corporate training programs, individuals with special needs, and those who want to use technology as a tool for learning.

State University of New York

The State University of New York (SUNY) unit of University Colleges of Technology has been actively working toward online delivery of courses since August 1996 as a natural progression from its existing distance learning program. It currently offers 14 courses online.

The faculty from each of the five schools in New York are developing courses that will allow anyone with Internet access to complete a degree in Computer Information Systems. (This will be extended to a bachelor's degree in Information Technology by early 2000.) Additionally, SUNY is developing the supporting courses students need to complete outside their major. The support courses are general study, mathematics, science, and electives. Extending online education to support courses will provide the flexibility to rapidly expand online education programs to other degree offerings.

The colleges offer degree and professional training programs that are accredited and certified by national academic and professional organizations. SUNY's specialized professional faculty serve as a resource for transferring their professional expertise to local, state, national, and international audiences in the areas of technology, agriculture, business, industry, health care, and science. The faculty also work with administration to help provide the same requirements and educational experience a student would have with an on-campus setting.

SUNY online courses are developed using TopClass software, which is an authoring tool that allows faculty to create courses with templates that help them navigate the development process. The SUNY project is funded through the SUNY Learning Network, which assists with the development of courses, marketing, registration, and help desk services for enrolled students. The cost for developing the 14 courses currently offered was $53,000. This included software licenses, technology, and faculty fees. The cost to the student is $99 per credit hour for New York State residents and $208 per credit hour for out-of-state residents.

The team at SUNY believes the future will involve aggressive approaches to incorporating streaming multimedia into Internet courses and programming. This will provide faculty with better means for developing and delivering online courses with improved retention by the participants.

University Summary

Associations can use these university online education models as springboards for their own programs. It is important to note that as universities seek out increased revenues and as the demand for education increases, they will aggressively seek new target audiences. For associations, this poses both an opportunity and a threat. The potential exists for associations to partner with universities to offer their members training programs designed by a university, saving time and money. There also is the potential for associations to lose their stronghold as the knowledge source for their members.

Associations

The scan data for associations were collected from March 1, 1998, to July 15, 1998.

This section focuses on three associations and the methods they used to approach online education. The American Society of Association Executives, the Canadian Society of Association Executives, and the American Association for Clinical Chemistry, Inc., are three among many associations that have become key players by aggressively delivering instruction to their members online.

Each of these organizations began by making fundamental development decisions about its program. These issues should be considered by all associations that wish to deliver online education. Associations should determine:

- Whether to make or buy—The association must decide whether a program or content should be developed in-house or purchased from an outside source. Considerations include the education strategy, available budget, staff to create internally, and, if a course or content exists from an outside source, its fit with existing education or training objectives.

- The degree of customization—A course developed in-house can be matched with any number of presentation methods, including discussion boards, interactive databases, audio, video, etc. A course or content purchased outside of the association often comes with the ability to private label the content, but may have limited ability to be enhanced with presentation features.

To highlight these options, the development decision process can be channeled into three approach methods. It is important to note that an approach method is unique to an association's online education strategy; no one approach is better than another. Also, associations tend to use a combination of these approaches.

- Approach Method A—Courses provided by an outside vendor with minor customization; courses involve minimal interactivity.

- Approach Method B—Courses provided by an outside vendor with part of the development work done by the association; courses involve a moderate level of interactivity.

- Approach Method C—Courses provided by the association or outside vendor, with most or all of the development work done by the association; courses use the latest technology applications for interactivity and multimedia.

The American Society of Association Executives
Education URL: www.asaenet.org/Education/Desktop/index.html
Approach Method A—Courses provided by an outside vendor with minor customization; courses involve minimal interactivity.

The American Society of Association Executives (ASAE) is dedicated to enhancing the professionalism and competency of association executives, promoting excellence in association management, and increasing the effectiveness of associations to better serve members and society.

ASAE offers its members and nonmembers the DesktopASAE education program with a virtual campus (VCampus) environment. Within the VCampus, users may select from a variety of Web-based courses, including courses in general management, telecommunications, ethics, Microsoft Access, and effective meetings.

ASAE focuses on association education anytime, anywhere, in virtually any setting by providing two formats: instructor-led courses and self-paced modules. Instructor-led courses are two to three weeks in length. Self-paced modules are computer-mediated, and they are shorter in length than the instructor-led seminars.

With an average of 30 users currently taking a course, DesktopASAE has been successful for many reasons. Some successful elements include:

- Clear online instructions that help users understand how to use the program and how to register are provided.

- Courses are open to both members and nonmembers, illustrating the association's dedication to education.

- User feedback is actively solicited and applied.

- Approximately 20 staff hours per week are devoted to program administration and the ongoing search for new and applicable courses to benefit associations.

Course development and user costs vary depending on the source of content, method of delivery, and complexity. A user's course cost ranges from $10 to $300. A large cost variable is linked to ASAE's decision to use self-paced modules developed by an outside developer, University Online (UOL). UOL has a library of over 350 courses. ASAE private labels its selection of titles from UOL within its VCampus environment. With the UOL agreement, there is the potential for an annually renewable contract to cover ASAE's selection of courses with no development costs involved.

ASAE's online education objectives are set to build on its two years of experience and include: delivering quality, cost-effective, accessible Web-based courses that focus primarily on association management, general leadership, and personal effectiveness; and exploring the conversion of traditional seminars for online delivery. ASAE's online education goal is to be the premier provider of professional association training. It is pursuing this goal by continually exploring delivery platforms and environments, including the range of technology—from telephone seminars to Web-based education (including asynchronous and synchronous) and developing technologies.

Canadian Society of Association Executives
Association URL: www.associationplace.com.
Approach Method B—Courses provided by an outside vendor with part of the development work done by the association; courses involve a moderate level of interactivity.

The Canadian Society of Association Executives (CSAE) provides targeted education for association managers. CSAE is dedicated to promoting excellence and best practices within association management and the association community. It delivers education programs to members through its Association Management Education Program (AME On-line).

AME On-line centers on current association management competencies. It provides management development courses that are delivered at a graduate level to association managers. The program serves the complex and diverse needs of the association community through five courses. These require candidates to complete research and assignments specific to their association of choice. Where permitted, the work of the candidates is used to contribute to the overall association management database, thus strengthening its relevance and currency.

Delivery via the Internet in itself presents a technology-learning opportunity. Course work and materials are computer based. The program demands interaction with others and the exchange of ideas and information. Instructors for each course provide support and ensure material is pertinent by updating course information via a system of templates. Because instructors are able to update course material themselves, staff time required to maintain the course is minimal.

AME On-line was launched with a major overhaul of course material in 1997 and is updated as needs emerge. The program consists of five online education courses that are based on association management competencies:

- AM100—Association Leadership, Change, Strategy, and Structure
- AM200—Association Membership Services
- AM300—Association Operations I (Operations Support)
- AM400—Association Operations II (Products and Services)
- AM500—Developments in Association Management

Courses are presented in lesson modules and focus on one or more competency subdomains. Each lesson has specific learning objectives and is easily adaptable by the instructor to reflect changing conditions. CSAE delivers six semesters per year, with an average of 50 candidates per semester. To date, more than 500 people have completed an AME course.

The evaluation process does not involve course exams. Course grading is based on completion of major assignments and participation in addressing questions and in researching issues specific to an association of choice. Although there is no formal evaluation process in place for participant response, feedback from participants has been very positive. This feedback has led to courses being developed and offered in multiple languages.

Successful elements of AME On-line include:

- Participants receive a certificate of completion that is recognized throughout the association community.
- Courses are based on association management competencies.
- Academic content of the program is relevant to associations.

- Instructors are seasoned association professionals who are able to facilitate learning and provide needed support.

- The program delivers practical tools and practices that can be used to address association management challenges.

- Participants have a unique opportunity to network electronically.

- Online discussions and assignments allow participants to draw on the experience of others, to apply the acquired knowledge to their associations, to identify best practices, and to share common challenges and network for enriched learning experiences.

CSAE continues to explore new online learning opportunities.

The American Association for Clinical Chemistry, Inc.
Association URL: www.aacc.org
Approach Method C—Courses provided by the association or outside vendor, with most or all of the development work done by the association; courses use the latest technology applications for interactivity and multimedia.

The American Association for Clinical Chemistry, Inc., (AACC) is an international scientific/medical society of clinical laboratory professionals, physicians, research scientists, and other individuals involved with clinical chemistry and other clinical laboratory science-related disciplines.

AACC has positioned itself as a leading resource for training not only in the scientific industry, but also in the association industry by training more than 4,000 people online in multiple countries since 1996. Examples of its courses include: The New ADA Guidelines, Tools to Improve Diabetes Test Management, Quality Control Planning, and Understanding the Clinical Uses of Blood Gases and Electrolytes. Several of AACC's courses are accessible for viewing without a password at the URL listed above.

Based on the level of dedication that AACC has devoted to online education, responses from users of its program have been positive:

"This should be clearly publicized to the general public as well as the scientific community."

"This was an excellent presentation and I will recommend it to my co-workers."

"This is the first online course that I have experienced. I enjoyed the variety of the text, the slides and the Q&A section. This was really an easy way to take the course."

"The content is excellent even for a professional who works outside of USA. It helps to implement a program or evaluate our actual situation of diabetes control. I like better the text presentation rather than the slide presentation."

AACC has built its program on a solid foundation. By incorporating the Internet and online education strategy into its organization's business plan, and continually improving and expanding its course offerings, AACC has experienced a high return rate as members return for more instruction. Also related to its online education strategy, AACC's high numbers of users are inversely related to the amount of staff time required to maintain the program. AACC reports that once a program goes live, it takes very little staff time to maintain.

Development and administrative costs for online courses have been low compared to costs associated with traditional courses due, in part, to the cost-effective benefits of technology, such as online registration. Promotional costs also have been reduced with the use of online brochures, broadcast faxes, and e-mails. Many of its programs are offered for free. However, there is a charge for certificate courses.

Some successful elements of AACC's online education program include:

- the use of advanced applications, including audio, video, and conferencing;
- the use of experienced instructors who work at building instructor–student rapport;
- the use of detailed needs assessments and evaluations;
- establishment of budgetary goals;
- affordable programs;
- the provision of continuing education credits;
- effective marketing through mass electronic communication;
- the application of users' feedback to future programs; and
- the use of a course rating system (basic, intermediate, advanced) to ensure proper application of the course material to the user.

Association Summary

A majority of the associations scanned and interviewed for this study use development approach method A. Solid training courses that require little additional effort on the part of the association are increasingly available from for-profit corporations, universities, and software vendors. These can help associations quickly develop an online offering.

Many associations simply "buy" the program through a vendor; only a few are more involved in program development. Also, the overall level of commitment tends to be higher as the level of in-house development increases.

The question associations must ask early on is: How will an approach method fit with the existing education strategy? Once this issue is resolved, the development process should move smoothly to the next level.

Corporations

The scan data for corporations were collected from March 1, 1998, to July 15, 1998.

Hewlett Packard (HP), Dow Chemical Company, and AutoDesk are three corporations that provide in-depth online training programs for their employees, with an eye on future expansion by training people outside their organization. Considering the corporate fiscal responsibility for expansion, it is possible that the corporate online education model will eventually seek revenue increases from markets that overlap with associations' markets. Because of this potential for overlap, associations must be aware of the corporate level of commitment to online education and be willing to learn from corporate online education models.

Hewlett Packard

Company URL: education.hp.com

HP offers free online seminars and Web-based training modules to benefit information technology (IT) professionals worldwide. These seminars and modules cover topics such as networks, system administration management, and leading technologies and are updated frequently.

HP is positioning itself as a training partner to help individuals and businesses realize the potential of their IT investments, using on-site, self-paced, and Web-based training options. HP believes in a comprehensive, customized education solution to help build a positive environment, reinforced by training the right people at the right time. By targeting all levels of an organization, from executives to front-line professionals, it believes the attitude and skills required to work successfully in this new environment are developed. HP has a training curriculum of more than 150 courses delivered at over 270 locations worldwide, with delivery options including on-site, self-paced, and online courses. Courses cover a wide range of technology areas, including UNIX, Microsoft, HP technologies, and Internet/intranet.

HP's ability to provide online training seminars and modules at no charge within its mix of training options positions it as a solid corporate benchmark.

Dow Chemical Company

Company URL: www.dow.com/homepage/index.html

Dow Chemical Company is the fifth largest chemical company in the world, with annual sales of more than $20 billion. It invests in over one million hours of training to 40,000 employees around the globe, leading to annual training expenses of $80 million.

Dow has been reviewing new methods of delivering training to help cut costs, including computer-based training and video. Because it needs constant updates, international requirements, and flexibility, Dow has determined that a Web-based training (WBT) model would best fit its needs. Although the process to convert existing educational content to the WBT format is extensive, Dow predicts this cost-saving online education project will produce a strong return on investment in just 18 months.

Dow is working with WBT Systems Inc., a developer of WBT software, to convert more than 600,000 hours of existing training materials to the Web format. The process started by converting materials in MS PowerPoint and MS Word; the project team is currently working on incorporating Web components, such as interactive applets, audio, and video, to converted materials. In addition to helping Dow convert its existing training to its intranet, WBT Systems is hosting Dow's ongoing training program.

Dow has used the results from extensive research to substantiate its decision to move to online education to more effectively reach its global audience while cutting overall training costs. Its decision to move away from the more traditional training models makes a strong case for associations to offer online education.

AutoDesk

Company URL: www.autodesk.com

AutoDesk is the fourth-largest PC software company worldwide and a global leader in design solutions and visualization. AutoDesk provides software applications that are widely used in many industries. These applications include geographic information systems, mechanical engineering, architecture, engineering, construction, and 3-D animation.

As it has advanced its educational programs, AutoDesk has created an a la carte menu with a variety of online learning resources and technical assistance. Items on this menu include self-paced courses, online extensions to the Autodesk Learning Assistance series, pretests, downloadable lessons, learning objectives, exercises, an authorized training center finder, access to product support information, and other resources and services to help participants become more productive users of AutoDesk products.

To help increase the general level of knowledge of educators and students worldwide about AutoDesk products, AutoDesk allows organizations to place a link on their Web site to AutoDesk's Education by Design site. The site is designed to help people in the worldwide educational community better handle the challenges that emerging technology may pose. The site encourages interactivity with its audiences. Site visitors learn about design software, trends in education, and what innovative educators and students are doing with their software.

AutoDesk is a strong example of a major corporation that is reaching beyond the limits of just providing instruction or education software. It is working to increase productivity and expand the general knowledge base of anyone in its area of expertise.

Corporation Summary

Corporate investment in online education and its affect on associations can be summed up by the following comments by Colin C. Rorrie, Jr., CAE, executive director of the American College of Emergency Physicians: "We don't have the exclusive province in education…. I think it's an area where we will see a lot of for-profit corporations actively competing with us."

The field of play in education has dramatically changed, and many players are scrambling to define their new roles. While training and education have been the franchise of associations and universities for many years, we can no longer rely on this outdated paradigm.

Today's corporations are operating in a world where "how training is conducted" has been dramatically affected by the need for faster learning curves. Flatter organizations require driving knowledge throughout the organization, while global marketplaces are expanding the distance students must travel. In this environment, seminars, academic courses, and other traditional training models are becoming increasingly outmoded.

This environment of change also has redefined the concept of who needs to be trained. New business models are based on supply chain partnerships sharing knowledge and working closely to add value to their products and services while simultaneously lowering costs and increasing speed to market. This requires moving outside the walls of training employees and extending coursework and knowledge to suppliers, marketing channels, and even customers.

To address their need to provide both knowledge and training quickly, frequently, in a customized format, and beyond the traditional walls, a growing number of corporations have entered the education and training arena. They have developed both in-house capabilities and external partnerships—whatever is the most effective at meeting their needs. Online education is increasingly becoming part of this solution. It has provided a way for corporations to reach their global audience, minimize involvement costs, and improve value through increased interactivity, assessment testing, and community building.

The implications for associations are clear:

- Corporations represent the entire spectrum of online education. Some have partnered with universities to repackage existing programs, while others have developed highly interactive programs using proprietary content that is rich with multimedia.

- If your association is to continue to be part of your members' education and training options, you will need to explore new ways of reaching out to them, which better matches their training needs.

- Knowledge sharing at even the lowest levels of an organization will become more critical. This will create new and more users of your information and training base as organizations drive decision making lower into their structure.

- New partnerships are being forged between corporations and other learning organizations, and associations need to be part of this new dynamic.

As more corporations begin to train and educate their overall value chain and customer base through online education, they can easily become your competition.

Depending on your association's education strategy, capabilities, and membership environment, you will need to decide which is the correct migration path to online education. But migrate you must.

Software Vendors

The scan data for software vendors were collected from March 1, 1998, to July 15, 1998.

Software vendors working in the education industry today are playing a key role in supporting online training programs offered by universities, associations, and corporations. With the online education market in its infancy, many software vendors are playing the role of both developer/manufacturer and service provider. Many software vendors are finding that it takes time to build distribution channels. During this start-up period, software vendors must provide direct service support to facilitate the end-user market.

Software vendors provide "tools"—the software programs necessary to create and deliver education across the training spectrum. Software vendors present associations with a wide variety of options for the development and delivery of online education, as well as a degree of dependency on the technology they provide.

To help build an understanding of how software vendors go about the business of providing online education solutions, it helps to have knowledge of the terminology they use in the marketplace. By knowing a few of the more common terms used by vendors and how they relate to familiar association development terms, you will have a head start on the eventual process of comparing and contrasting software vendors offering programs that appear very similar:

- Preauthoring—Instructional designers use this to move from the starting point through the initial stages of an online program. (The analysis and design phases are considered preauthoring.)

- Authoring—This focuses on the middle stages of an online program, following the initial stages and before delivering a program. (The development phase is commonly referred to as authoring.)

- Evaluation—This allows for the validation of elements developed and for course testing. (This term also is commonly used by associations to refer to the same stage of development.)

- Management—This provides program registration, data handling, reporting, learning profiles, and more. (This term also is commonly used by associations to refer to the same stage of development.)

- Courseware—This is a product or group of products that helps organizations create and deliver an online training program. (The analysis, design, development, evaluation, and management phases all may be created using courseware.)

To assess software vendors who provide online education that involves using a specific tool or set of courseware, associations need to begin by conducting some research on the subject. The objective with this research is to narrow the field to those vendors who provide a solution that matches the association's online education strategy. The appendices at the back of this guide provide useful information on this topic:

- Appendix B features sample vendor fact report information; you will find it useful when benchmarking or discussing options with a vendor.

- Appendix C contains scan information of vendors who provide full-line solutions. "Full-line" is defined as software tools that facilitate most or all of an organization's online training objectives.

- Appendix D contains information on vendors who provide specialized solutions. "Specialized" is defined as software tools that facilitate specific aspects of an organization's training objectives.

Software Vendor Summary

As with any developing marketplace, there are a variety of methods vendors use to approach the market. Software vendors who produce products to facilitate online programs have distinctive approaches including:

- The production of software tools that facilitate the complete spectrum of online education, from asynchronous to synchronous delivery.

- The production of software tools that facilitate only certain components of online education, such as testing or management.

- The production of software tools that can be used to support online education, such as chat forums, but that have many uses beyond just online education.

Associations are not likely to find consistency with software pricing in the current market, because of evolving business models and varying distribution approaches. Research conducted during this study found that the industry supports multiple pricing methods, including pricing by the number of registered online users, licensing fees for open use, and simple purchase programs. To learn more about software pricing, see Appendix B, which contains pricing information from select vendors.

Case studies are presented here to provide key advice from selected associations on their experience with online education. These case studies illustrate the actual experiences associations have had with online education ventures, with each association featured working at a different level to provide online instruction to members. The organizations featured here represent a cross-section of the associations studied. Their stories help to illustrate an understanding of key issues that face associations at various stages in the development, delivery, and management processes. Each organization selected is unique, but their experiences with offering online courses can be helpful to other associations.

In chapter 2, online education approach methods used by associations were introduced; they are repeated here based on their relevance for benchmarking the associations featured in the case studies. It is important to note again that a development approach is unique to an association's online education strategy; no one approach is better than another. Associations also tend to use a combination of these approaches.

- Approach Method A—Courses provided by an outside vendor with minor customization; courses involve minimal interactivity.

- Approach Method B—Courses provided by an outside vendor with part of the development work done by the association; courses involve a moderate level of interactivity.

- Approach Method C—Courses provided by the association or outside vendor, with most or all of the development work done by the association; courses use the latest technology applications for interactivity and multimedia.

Each case study is presented in the following format: profile, program overview, primary goals, strategies, cost/price issues, top challenges, best practices, and success measures.

Association of Public Health Laboratories

Association URL: www.aphl.org
Approach Method A—Courses provided by an outside vendor with minor customization; courses involve minimal interactivity.

Profile

The Association of Public Health Laboratories' (APHL) mission is to promote the role of public health laboratories in support of national and global health objectives, and to promote policies and programs that ensure continuous improvement in the quality of laboratory practice. APHL works on behalf of public health laboratories as an advocate through legislation, policy development, public information, environmental health issues, and public health surveillance systems.

Program Overview

APHL is unique with respect to the number of professionals it trains per year: approximately 7,000 in a traditional environment. APHL realized that it needed to use technology to effectively grow and offer more content-rich programs to this large number of people who need continuing education.

Primary Goals

APHL's primary goal is to continue to institute quality educational programs that are accessible and affordable for members. It believes that the bells and whistles of technology won't be the driving force, but quality will and that good instructional design must be adhered to in all cases. Another major goal is to develop partnerships with other organizations that have a good "fit" with APHL to strengthen online offerings.

Strategies

APHL conducts frequent training needs assessments, including surveys, to determine the technological capacity of members to receive online courses. APHL also uses the most competent faculty for each course. The credentials of the faculty are less important to APHL than technical competency. The field of public health laboratory science demands that member laboratorians always be afforded the most up-to-date techniques to fulfill APHL's vision of "a healthier world through quality laboratory practice."

Cost/Price Issues

The costs involved in the initial development of the APHL course were related mostly to instructional design, honoraria for the faculty, advertising, printing of brochures, mailings, printing of certificates, clerical assistance, Web server charges, and hosting fees. The programmer that developed the program was outside APHL and customized several "off the shelf" software applications to arrive at the final application. APHL charged $20 to members of the co-sponsoring nonprofit and $25 for nonmembers, and gave them an option of paying $35 to become a member of the co-sponsoring nonprofit group and take the seminar.

Registration fees for each course average about $50. The development costs for a traditional workshop depend on speaker availability, distance traveled, the number of speakers, location, and the need for renting specialized equipment, such as microscopes. Generally, a budget is developed first, and then the registration is set with the intent of at least breaking even.

Because APHL is small and funding is limited for unrestricted activities, it tends to work closely with funding sources to identify areas of mutual interest with regard to online education. Communication with members and funding sources concerning their respective needs is key to moving ahead with online education.

Top Challenges

APHL identified the following challenges:

- Getting others to understand that the association must take chances. APHL leadership feels that APHL must make online education an option, even if not every member has electronic access. It believes that technology is becoming more accessible and that the association should lead the way.

- Finding the funding and time. Because of a limited budget, APHL must be innovative in its approach to online education by using resources and staff wisely. Down the road that may mean establishing relationships with the corporate/supplier community to help fund new initiatives.

- Resolving technical concerns. This includes solving problems with the server and overcoming limitations with software.

Best Practices

APHL concentrates on conducting needs assessments with members. By understanding the needs and level of technological competence, APHL designs programs that meet the training needs of the target audience.

Success Measures

APHL uses the following to measure the success of its programs:

- Volume of students accessing online training

- Student evaluations upon completion of the course

- Evidence of impact, or a change in behavior and technique as a result of the course

- Programs that not only break even, but generate funds that can be used to develop additional training resources

American College of Healthcare Executives

Association URL: www.ache.org

Approach Method B—Courses provided by an outside vendor with part of the development work done by the association; courses involve a moderate level of interactivity.

Profile

The American College of Healthcare Executives (ACHE) is an international professional society of nearly 30,000 healthcare executives. ACHE is known for its prestigious credentials and educational programs. It is also known for its *Journal of Healthcare Management* and magazine, *Healthcare Executive*, as well as ground-breaking research, career development, and public policy programs. ACHE strives to improve the health status of society by advancing healthcare management excellence.

Program Overview

ACHE features two online learning programs: the Virtual Congress on Healthcare Management and online education seminars. The Virtual Congress supports educational events for healthcare executives by incorporating audio (real audio), printed script of audio, and copies of slides. Seminars allow participants to interact through the members-only area of the ACHE homepage using the case study approach. Working at their own pace, participants discuss information related to healthcare management issues and may earn education credits.

Primary Goal

The primary goal for ACHE's online education program is to provide an additional resource for healthcare professionals to gain needed instruction and information.

Strategies

ACHE continues to pursue methods of making its education more accessible to healthcare professionals by promoting online education to members and nonmembers and providing online registration with payment processing to help facilitate enrollments.

Cost/Price Issues

For the Virtual Congress on Healthcare Management ACHE offers four, 90-minute sessions, for a total of six hours of instruction, and charges members $300. The cost for developing the online courses has been minimal to date because the courses make use of material from existing traditional programs.

Top Challenges

ACHE's major challenge is to increase members' use of the Web to take courses offered. ACHE is working on target marketing of mailing information to help improve and increase member online activity.

Best Practices

The Virtual Congress on Healthcare Management represents ACHE's most significant development to date by taking advantage of cutting-edge technology. The program allows participants to register online, complete the program at their own pace, conduct a self-test to assess retention, and complete an online evaluation. ACHE also offers a toll-free help line, which allows participants to contact staff to ask questions.

Success Measures

The success measures for ACHE's online education programs include:

- Overall program evaluation as assessed by participants
- Increase in the nondues revenue stream—ACHE expects online programs to break even or generate a positive return
- Attendance—Attendance targets are established, monitored, and then reassessed

Special Libraries Association

Association URL: www.sla.org
Approach Method B—Courses provided by an outside vendor with part of the development work done by the association; courses involve a moderate level of interactivity.

Profile

The Special Libraries Association (SLA) is an international association representing the interests of nearly 15,000 information professionals in 60 countries. Special librarians are information resource experts who collect, analyze, evaluate, package, and disseminate information to facilitate accurate decision-making in corporate, academic, and government settings.

Program Overview

In addition to internal, self-paced programs, SLA has partnered with a major university to position its online training and learning programs as a priority. This strategy is based on interaction with customers and targeted focus groups. With many choices of programs suitable for online learning, SLA listens to its potential students to develop the most appropriate content for delivery in this medium. It has achieved success by establishing and following strict program guidelines.

Primary Goals

Goals for online education at SLA are the same as the overall strategic plan. The mission of this plan is to ensure that members have ample opportunity to develop their professional competencies and skills and to transition them to a virtual association whereby all members will be able to access SLA services globally, equitably, and continuously.

Strategies

SLA does extensive research before implementing any type of online educational program. This includes exploring educational technology, by asking questions such as: How does the technology work? What are the advantages and disadvantages? Which curriculum is best suited to this type of programming? For example, with the asynchronous courses it offers, SLA partners with a university. SLA staff not only researched asynchronous education and what it entails, but also participated in one of the partner university's courses presented in this manner before offering this type of program to members. In addition, SLA looks at the professional development program as a whole. It asks: Which courses really need to be taught in person? Which current courses could be converted to an online format? It then determines the areas that would be a good fit for the online format (i.e., a course on Web-page design).

Cost/Price Issues

SLA keeps development costs down by using courses from an outside developer when possible. SLA pays a developer a per-person fee of $195, which includes registering the students, teaching the course, and providing all the materials that each student will need. SLA then charges members $310 to take the course. The cost for a self-paced online course developed by SLA is about $1,000 for the content and about $2,500 to $3,000 to have each course designed for an interactive format. In comparison, the development of an in-person intensive institute costs a total of about $25,000. SLA expects a six-month return on investment on the total training development expenditures over the past year.

SLA also offers a full-day continuing education (CE) course to members for $205. Two- to three-day CE programs cost members an average of $400 to $450. SLA's most expensive CE program is $1,250; this program is for a very specific audience of senior-level members.

Top Challenges
Though SLA wants to move forward and offer more online education in striving to be a virtual association, there are limitations to what can be accomplished given the number of staff in the Professional Development department. One way SLA has met this challenge is to take a close look at what programs are already in place to see if there are any that can be reformatted for the Web. Next, SLA has explored partnerships with universities and related professional associations. Fortunately, SLA was able to find a reputable university with which to partner. Taking these steps has enabled SLA to save staff time and budget dollars. Though SLA has had success in both of these areas, it is finding that for the online education program to grow, it needs to develop additional programs from the ground up, which will require a great deal of staff time.

SLA's greatest operational challenge has been establishing procedures to ensure the smooth execution of the online education programs. The Professional Development department partners with other departments, such as Accounting and Computer Services, to provide online education. Working together as a team in these areas, SLA staff have been able to develop new procedures for these courses and extensions, such as registering for courses, accessing courses on the Web site, and troubleshooting.

Best Practices
The most significant management best practice from SLA's online education experience has been the association's willingness to stretch and go beyond what it had been accustomed to offering members. The first time SLA provided online education to the membership was a risk; there were no guarantees that members would buy into this type of program. SLA members do value the online education they receive and are asking for more of these types of activities.

The most significant operational best practice is ensuring the smooth delivery of programs from the start. Since online education was new to members, it was vital that their first experience be successful. Though the content of the course must be high quality, how it is presented to the members makes the difference as to whether they will choose to enroll in future online programs.

Success Measures

One of the biggest measures of success in the first year is whether the organization follows through with presenting the first online educational offering from beginning to end. Though many associations have good intentions of presenting this type of program to their members, the program may never get off the ground because of lack of knowledge on how to go about it, budget constraints, or fear that members are not ready for this type of program. SLA was excited to move beyond these barriers and presented the first online educational offering to members in 1997. This in itself was a measure of success. Following the completion of the first year of conducting online education, SLA interviewed members who participated in the courses. To help measure the success of the program, SLA asked questions such as:

- How do you feel about online education?

- Would you take a similar course in the future?

- What didn't you like about it?

- What are some suggestions to improve the presentation of material in this format?

Association of Public-Safety Communications Officials International, Inc.

Association URL: www.apcointl.org

Approach Method C—Courses provided by the association or outside vendor, with most or all of the development work done by the association; courses use the latest technology applications for interactivity and multimedia.

Profile

The Association of Public-Safety Communications Officials International (APCO) is the world's oldest and largest nonprofit professional organization dedicated to the enhancement of public safety communications. With more than 13,000 members worldwide, APCO exists to serve the people who manage, operate, maintain, and supply the communications systems used to safeguard the lives and property of citizens everywhere.

Program Overview

APCO Institute currently has eight courses available online that are scheduled throughout the year. APCO created the Institute to manage all education and training issues and a Virtual Institute for classes that are available over the World Wide Web. Staff attribute much of the success of online programs to aggressive and unique marketing efforts. The Virtual Institute was launched with a promotional campaign that featured "Good for One Free" tuition certificates to member agencies. Encouraged by the participants' positive experiences, others from their agencies have since enrolled in Virtual Institute courses.

Primary Goal

The primary goal of the Virtual Institute is to provide public safety communications professionals with an additional way to receive education and training beyond traditional methods of delivery.

Strategies

To achieve this goal, APCO Institute aggressively markets to all levels of the public safety community, from the front-line call taker to the various levels of management, and tries to not exclude professionals at any level with technology they cannot access.

Cost/Price Issues

The cost of developing an online course is slightly higher than the cost of developing a traditional course. For example, the development cost for a traditional 40-hour course is approximately $12,000. An additional $800 expense is incurred when preparing the same material for online presentation. The additional cost represents roughly 10 percent of the original cost. The extra costs are attributed to 16 hours of additional development at $50 per development hour. APCO charges the same tuition for courses, regardless of whether they are offered in traditional or Web-based format. APCO estimates traditional course development to be 10 development hours per hour of instruction at $50 per development hour. All of its courses are then priced at the same rate as a standard classroom course presentation. Thresholds are established to determine the break-even point of the course to the cost paid to the instructor and Web site maintenance fees.

Top Challenges

Marketing is one of the top challenges. Once the student is involved in online learning, that student should keep coming back for more. The challenge is getting the initial student.

APCO has not experienced any significant operational challenges. The biggest operational challenge to date was changing webmasters and servers at the same time. This caused "much aggravation," but every effort was made to maintain operational performance with minimal impact to the students and the classes in progress.

Best Practices

APCO conducts a front-end analysis of the audience and keeps the technology used in the program simple and accessible. While APCO Institute has the ability to do many things with courses (pushing audio/video, etc.), the audience does not have the necessary computing power to use these bells and whistles. APCO Institute designed and operates the Virtual Institute to bring education and training to an audience that may not otherwise be able to attend training and education. This format provides work centers the flexibility to train their employees without disrupting personnel schedules and eliminates costs involved in paying for travel, overtime, and per diem expenses.

Success Measures

The first measure of success was the feedback from participants. The feedback received was encouraging and led to an expanded program of eight courses. Initially, APCO tested two courses by inviting individuals with various levels of computer knowledge to participate. APCO also projected an in-house tentative schedule for a few months out should the test course be well received. No other information was made public. The third week into the test courses, several tentatively scheduled courses were filled, with no advertising or promotions.

The other measure of success was from peers. This came in the form of the ASAE Award for Technology-Based Education Programs for 1997.

The American Association for Clinical Chemistry, Inc.

Association URL: www.aacc.org

Approach Method C—Courses provided by the association or outside vendor, with most or all of the development work done by the association; courses use the latest technology applications for interactivity and multimedia.

Profile

The American Association for Clinical Chemistry, Inc., (AACC) is an international scientific/medical society of clinical laboratory professionals, physicians, research scientists, and other individuals involved with clinical chemistry and other clinical laboratory science-related disciplines.

Program Overview

AACC is a veteran in the online education business, with over 4,000 people trained in multiple countries since 1996. It offers educational and informational programs in the scientific arena. AACC credits its high return rate to the use of many enabling technologies, its close watch on success measures, and its seasoned instructors who build strong instructor/student rapport.

Primary Goal

The primary goal of online education at AACC is to provide timely, high-quality educational programs on topics important to members in a manner that is cost effective and convenient to the end user.

Strategies

Educational topics at AACC are evaluated for both need and format. Presenters are carefully chosen and trained as to the differences between online education and other formats so that they can help develop a high-quality presentation. Budgets and promotional plans are drafted and managed. AACC works to apply what it has learned in past programs to continually improve future online offerings.

Cost/Price Issues

For AACC, online program development costs are less expensive than development costs for traditional courses. Some costs associated with traditional courses, such as travel costs, facility costs, or audio conference telephone charges, are not incurred in online courses. Registration administrative costs are less than those for traditional courses because attendees register online. Promotional costs are also considerably less because online brochures, broadcast faxes, and e-mail messages are used, rather than traditional print-and-mail pieces.

The cost to the users of online courses varies with the program. Several AACC programs have been offered for free to participants. In general, AACC charges for more substantial self-study-type courses that lead to a certificate.

Top Challenges

The major challenge for AACC was getting through the logistics and technology of the first program. Each program is built using past programs as a foundation and is continuously improved. The first program used an outside vendor for hardware and support. All other programs have used in-house hardware and support. AACC says it was surprising how easy it was to bring the project in-house.

Best Practices

AACC attributes much of its online education success to its approach: Firmly and quickly incorporate the Internet into the business plan and continually improve and expand existing programs.

Success Measures

AACC measures the success of its programs by examining the following:

- Attendance
- Evaluations
- Budgetary goals
- Fulfillment of continuing education needs assessment goals
- Programs that are accessible, affordable, and high quality
- New audiences

4. Best Practices

This section focuses on two key areas: (1) executive and operational management best practices of associations that currently provide online education, and (2) business planning tips.

Executive Management

- Begin by developing a business plan with a financial forecast.

- Online training activities must be central to an executive's financial thinking.

- Make sure key people are there at the end, by involving them at the onset of program design.

- Talk to other association leaders and members early in the process to see what worked for them.

- Establish who is responsible for each phase of the program, including a program manager, course editor or an editorial board, and a content expert.

- Carefully consider budget requirements for ongoing updates and improvements.

- Ask for program support from suppliers, instructors, and local boards. Then choose members to help champion the project.

Operational Management

- Conduct research to determine which programs are appropriate for an online format to help create a balanced education program. Consider creating a grid of all educational activities and plot which ones would best be offered as a conference, hands-on workshop, videoconference, roundtable, online course, etc.

- Consider the audience's expectations for a flexible structure, multiple support options, and fast response times during early development.

- Establish continuing education credits whenever possible to build course credibility.

- Consider the audience's learning requirements and technical capabilities carefully.

- With enough lead-time, pilot the program with a group of representative members to work out any glitches. After going live—the first 72 hours are critical—watch closely for student concerns.

- Train the trainers who present the course in both the material and technology.

- Advertise the program through both traditional and online efforts.

- Prepare membership for online education by explaining the rationale for providing this type of education, including the many advantages. Once they have decided to participate, let them know what to expect from the course, the requirements, and detailed instructions on how to participate.

Business Planning Tips

Before beginning any design or production work for online education, assess the audience, location, structure, content, goals of the event, needs of the stakeholders, and mission of the host organization. While meeting with the management team, discuss the following:

- Organizational mission

- Goals of the educational event to be broadcast on the Web

- Additional goals that should be set for the online event not previously identified

- Creation of a strategy to reach those goals

- Steps needed to be taken to meet the goals

- Who is responsible for each step

Stakeholders are people who have an interest in the development or broadcast of the online event. Determine who the stakeholders are for the event and review existing materials to gather pertinent information about them. Contact the stakeholders and conduct interviews or surveys to determine their needs. Incorporate the perceived or expressed needs of these stakeholders into the design of the online event. Stakeholders for online events may include:

- Association Executives—their vision of the association's role in online education

- Organization Members—profiles, expectations, and demographics

- Past and Current Students—registration, records from previous courses

- Sponsors—current sponsors and past sponsors of previous conferences, publications, or events and the target audiences for these sponsors

- Prospective Students—demographic information and profiles, including various subsets of viewers (i.e., members, prospective members, university professors, students, public)
- The Press—press releases, media plans, media contacts

Course Overview

The online course Effective Strategic Planning for Associations was developed to provide the association community with an innovative online educational model that was association tested, used emerging Web technology, was tested for student readiness and content, and reinforced the subject matter by emphasizing interactive and measurable learning.

This model for online education began with the following selections:

- The topic to be studied would be association strategic planning.

- The test group of participants would consist of the members of the American Association of Medical Society Executives (AAMSE).

- The instructor would be Ginger Nichols, an association expert in the field of strategic planning and president of GinCommGroup. Nichols volunteered her time, content, and objectives for the online course.

After the topic was selected, a survey was conducted with members of AAMSE; the survey was validated by the study's executive panel. After two months of development, the final course was delivered in two sessions over a three-week period ending November 30, 1998. Each session was developed using approach method C (using advanced technology applications and interactivity). The high level of technology and interactivity was selected specifically to provide a benchmark for associations using this model. The delivery of Session 1 was asynchronous, with interactive elements and the use of new technologies, such as JAVA script for online testing. Session 2 used a mix of both asynchronous and synchronous delivery, with advanced applications in a live interactive chat forum.

The work process, elements of the course map, evaluation criteria, and measures for success used for the online model course were developed from feedback by technical advisers, GinCommGroup, the executive panel, and Fusion Productions instructional designers; these elements were validated by the executive panel. Measures for success applied to the course included participant response, achievement of learning objectives, level of acceptance of the delivery method, and instructor response.

The rest of this chapter addresses the mapping process, course software capabilities, benchmark development and technical considerations, process checklist, and the result summary of the online course model.

The Mapping Process

A course map represents the sequential positioning of content and overall organization of course elements. A course map can provide:

- Visual cues of the content to the learner, such as what parts of the course have already been seen, or remain to be seen. This could include units, lessons, pretests, and post-tests, depending on the course structure.

- Learning dependencies, if any, such as a section of content that must be learned before another section. Organizing content this way requires that the course be logically and intuitively designed.

- Organization of production responsibilities during course development. Production team members can gauge the amount of work they're doing and how it fits into the entire course.

The elements that were designed and used for the online course are presented here first in outline form, and then in detail within instructional design categories. Each category, objective, content, testing, and evaluation, together with supporting information, has been adapted from instructional design standards to provide a useful representation of the mapping process used for the online course.

Course Map Outline

Introduction

Preassessment

Course overview

Session 1 overview

Prereading for Session 1

Session 1—Fundamentals of Strategic Planning for Associations

    Major benefits of engaging in strategic planning

    Skill Test One

    Assessing organizational readiness

    Organizing the strategic planning process

Conducting an environmental scan

Trends impacting associations

Prereading for Session 2

Session 2—Applications of Association Strategic Planning

Five steps in the strategic planning process

Skill Test Two

Formulating specific objectives and strategies

Why strategic plans may fail

How material presented relates to participants' association

Mastery Test

Course Evaluation

Course Map Detail
Objectives

The creation of instructionally sound objectives for content delivery is the first step in the process. Begin by creating objectives that match the existing online education business strategy, including stated goals, available budgets, etc. With a completed list of objectives in hand, list the objectives in a logical sequence, from start to finish. Finally, assign each objective to one or more areas of the course map (units, sessions, and tests). If an objective does not apply to the map, either it is unimportant or a place for the objective may need to be created.

Objectives used for sessions 1 and 2 of the online course included:

- Recognize the benefits of strategic planning

- Assess your organization's readiness for strategic planning

- Know how to organize a strategic planning process

- Understand the importance of an environmental scan

- Understand the steps used to conduct a strategic planning process

- Understand how to formulate specific objectives and strategies as part of the strategic planning process

- Recognize the common pitfalls of strategic plans and why they may fail

Content

Content generation and how it is applied to the course correlates closely with the steps in the objective process. Following the creation or adaptation of existing content, sequence the content in a natural progression, for example, from simple to complex. Take care at this point to match content to previously assigned objectives. Next, assign the content to the course map. Finally, match the content with a technology for delivery, such as a database form, PowerPoint slides, audio, video, etc.

Content used for sessions 1 and 2 of the online course included:

Session 1—Fundamentals of Strategic Planning for Associations
Prereading

Articles and material relating to fundamentals, to be read before starting Session 1:
- The Power of the Plan
- Key Definitions of Strategic Planning Terms
- Facing the Future: Preparing Your Association To Thrive

Major benefits of engaging in strategic planning

Instructor's notes include information about the benefits of conducting strategic planning and the need to develop a plan, such as who should participate, a planning schedule, and needed resources.

Assessing organizational readiness

Discussion board for threaded discussion on specific questions posed by instructor. Questions included:

1. Is there a champion on the board for the strategic planning process?
2. Do you have buy-in from key association leaders?
3. Do you have buy-in from senior staff?
4. Can you devote adequate time to the process, including research that may be needed for a comprehensive environmental scan?
5. Can you create a budget to support the process?
6. Is there an understanding among board and staff that strategic planning is not a one-time event but an ongoing process?

Organizing the strategic planning process

Discussion board for threaded discussion on a specific question posed by the instructor: If your association were to begin a strategic planning process today, who would you include on the planning team and why?

Conducting an environmental scan

The importance of conducting a detailed environmental scan before beginning the strategic planning process and continuing to conduct ongoing scans. Presented via video stream, with industry expert providing insight and examples.

Trends impacting associations

Discussion board for threaded discussion on association trends provided in the prereading material related to specific implications for participant's organization.

Session 2—Applications of Association Strategic Planning
Prereading

Articles and material relating to the application of strategic planning to an association, to be read before starting Session 2.
- The Paradoxes of Strategic Planning
- Avoiding Eight Pitfalls of Strategic Planning
- Learning How To Create the Future

Five steps in the strategic planning process

Instructor's notes include information and insight on five steps to follow when applying the process to an organization.

Formulating specific objectives and strategies

Review a case study online about an association that has implemented a strategic planning process, focusing on its posted objectives and strategies.

Why strategic plans may fail

Review considerations as to why strategic plans may fail. Present via PowerPoint slide show.

How material presented relates to participants' association

Live, instructor-led online chat conducted by instructor to focus on specific participant examples. Questions posed by instructor to begin discussion.

Testing

Test questions are usually found at the end of sessions or units, but may be freely assigned anywhere in the course map. The purpose is to select questions that will test participants' knowledge or skills that are specifically related to the session objectives or content. A clearly written objective can be the basis of several test questions. It is important to select enough questions to address a majority of the content covered to help avoid assessment gaps and to identify areas of weakness.

Testing areas used for the online course included:

Skill Tests—Skill tests are provided in sessions 1 and 2 to assess knowledge on content provided in prereading and instructor's notes. Uses game quiz show format with questions, immediate feedback, and suggested references.

Mastery Test—The mastery test is delivered online after the course is completed. The test is designed to measure learning objectives met. The online form includes true/false, multiple-choice, and open-ended questions.

Evaluation

Traditionally, a course is organized to present the concepts first, followed by an assessment. If the objective is simply to gather demographic data, this can be obtained when the participant registers, but if the objective is to evaluate participant response on content, then the use of a pretest, preassessment, post-test, or simulation is best. Position the data-gathering tool in an appropriate place in the course, such as before or after a session or unit. Doing this helps isolate the strengths and weaknesses of the participant and helps to prescribe a learning path that is best for that individual.

Evaluation tools used for the online course included:

Preassessment—Preassessment is delivered online before students start the course, via an online form to capture students' experience and capability. The information gathered is used to deliver appropriate information to students. For example, the instructor can learn that there are areas within the curriculum that should be stressed, while others may be skipped. The online form includes questions in the areas of professional experience, association information, and technical capabilities.

Course Evaluation—Course evaluation is delivered online after the mastery test is completed, via the online form. The results are used to determine whether the course objectives and the overall course goal have been met.

Course Software Capabilities

Allen Communications Designer's Edge courseware was selected for the initial phases of the AAMSE course development, also known as preauthoring. Designer's Edge provided a set of integrated tools and wizards to facilitate the instructional design process. From this initial phase, Designer's Edge helped the developers build a detailed storyboard and link directly to other advanced technology applications used for development and delivery including:

- Microsoft Front Page 98—HTML coding
- VIVO Player—viewing of streaming media
- O-Reilly Webboard—discussion board
- Java Script—interactive testing
- E-Share—interactive chat forum

Using a visual, task-driven interface, Designer's Edge is able to analyze a target audience, establish clear objectives, outline content, and select learning strategies. Allen Communications provides tools and services that facilitate the complete process of multimedia development including:

- Quest—authoring
- Designer's Edge—instructional design
- Net Synergy—HTML/Java Web delivery
- Manager's Edge—training delivery and management

Benchmark Development Considerations

Associations that deliver online education will at some point be required to address each of the following development and technical considerations. These considerations emerged from experience with the AAMSE online course. Associations can use this background to save time and money when developing online education. The development and technical considerations are presented in the following order within the developmental outline: analysis, design, development, evaluation, and management.

Analysis

- Ask targeted questions during analysis to best determine the audience's particular needs, including:

  - Previous experience with using personal computer and multimedia training

  - Preferred method of training (instructor led, independent study, computer based, Web based)

  - Computer and software capability (browser, RAM, etc.)

  - Experience with subject matter

- If the assessment indicates that the target audience is at varying levels of understanding, consider grouping participants according to level of understanding to increase results or offering a different level course targeted directly to each group.

Design

- Determine the most manageable, efficient number of students to place in each class or session. This will lead to realistic instructor time commitments, on- and off-line, and improved flow of online chats.

- Determine the level of interactivity needed between student/teacher, and student/student with the given content to keep the course on track with learning objectives.

- If the level of content difficulty or if the requirement for retention is high, create a pretest in addition to an assessment to more accurately determine the target audience's actual level of knowledge.

- Create testing questions to match the content or learning objective, thus increasing the opportunity for achieving the desired learning outcome.

Development

- Begin this phase of the project with a completed map from the design phase so that each department or team needed to complete the project will have a sound working knowledge base.

- Integrate entertainment into the program through the use of basic multimedia (graphics, animation, sound) to help maintain the students' interest.

- Have a clear method of communication between each group working on the project, including the instructional design team, graphics, technical, and program administrators, and use it to avoid lost time from rework.

Evaluation

- Explain testing components carefully, including how to use the component and the relationship of the participants' score or results to the course.

- Clearly match testing methodology and delivery to course learning objectives. If higher content retention is required, tests may be delivered via an online form to capture responses and conduct detailed evaluations.

- Ensure a mix of open- and closed-ended questions is presented in the course impact evaluations. This provides students the best opportunity to clearly state their feelings about the course, and for administrators to draw the best conclusions for learning outcomes and future course design.

Management

- Program management covers all phases of an online education course and hinges on effective communication. It is vital to communicate items learned with each group working on the course relative to its area of responsibility.

- Consider exactly how course data from evaluations, testing, and assessments will be used for reporting. The objective is to minimize work between the generation of data and clear reporting.

Benchmark Technical Considerations

Analysis

- Match a browser to the course to be delivered. Browsers are updated regularly and may not be able to support specific applications needed to deliver specific content. Choosing the correct browser to support your program is particularly important if the course contains advanced interactive applications. If the course has little or no interactivity and minimal multimedia, it is more likely that more or older browsers would work. Explain in detail to students how to download and install a free browser if necessary.

- Determine exactly what applications will be used with all phases of the program. Courseware tools are available for each phase of development, including this initial analysis phase. Detailed applications used for development and to enable technologies, such as chat and video streaming, are common as well.

Design

- Carefully consider the use of multiple enabling technologies, such as chat, discussion forums, video, and audio, in the same course. Using too many applications at the same time may result in less than positive experiences by students if they are not familiar with each application. Make sure the needs of the student come before the technology, because the technology can quickly become the focal point.

- Prioritize the graphical images and content on the screen so that students understand what is important and have enough working space with minimum scrolling.

- Ensure online chat forums have the least number of participants possible at one time. By conducting a chat with too many participants, the instructor will find it difficult to respond to questions input, and the students' attentions may drift.

- Keep online reading to a minimum, and provide the ability for students to print documents as a viewing alternative. If the amount of required reading is large, provide the reference as early as possible in the course to give students more time for reading and retention.

- Establish an operating protocol between the instructor and student when using communication software, including chat forums and discussion boards. This will reduce participant concern with using this form of communication and improve the interaction. For example, when establishing a chat forum, state at the start of a discussion that the current subject will be covered for 10 minutes, allowing participants to anticipate a shift to the next subject.

Development

- Minimize the use of hyperlinks to outside URLs to reduce the opportunity for a student to not come back.

- Carefully review online forms used for registration, assessment, testing, and evaluation after they are coded for online use. The process of converting standard text for use online creates the possibility for changes to the context originally intended by designers.

- When using multimedia, such as video and audio, use "streaming media" applications when possible to decrease the loading time on a student's system. Streaming applications allow students to begin viewing or listening to the desired media before it is completely downloaded to their system.

- Ensure there is detailed instructions for participants on how to use any plug-in applications that are incorporated into a course, including those that enable streaming media, discussion boards, and chat forums. These instructions should include each step of what the student is required to do (i.e., download and install a program) or what the student may expect to see happen on screen.

- Carefully consider connection speed and screen resolution during program development. It is common to develop a course for a low connection speed and a 640 x 480 screen resolution unless there is a clear understanding that the target audience's computer capabilities will permit more. An alternative is to design for multiple connection speeds to help match the capabilities of more target audiences.

Evaluation

- Use online forms to make testing (precourse, post-course, and during the course) more efficient. An online form will allow data to be captured in a digital file and then be used by a variety of common applications, such as Microsoft Word, for reporting.

- Test all course components created under as many real-life conditions as possible. This relates to the analysis phase and the expected system configurations and software the target audience will use.

- If JAVA script is used to deliver interactive tests, clearly state the system and browser requirements for conducting the test and what to expect on screen, such as increased load times.

Management

- Be consistent in requiring the use of a password and user name, if there is such a requirement to enter more than one section of the course. This will help reduce student confusion.

- Use a database to keep track of all information related to the course. This will help facilitate course management and provide a more unified approach to training as more courses are added to the overall program.

- Stress that server management is important to maintain control over internal and external course access, space requirements, and backups and to provide consistent technical support.

Process Checklist

The following process outline was used with the AAMSE online course. An association should create and follow a formal checklist to help ensure that each step in the process has been completed.

- ❑ Identify association staff responsible for each phase.

- ❑ Survey the target audience to determine its learning needs, computer platform capabilities, and the best instructional method to use (i.e., case studies, group discussion, etc.).

- ❑ Identify and obtain the required technology tools needed to create and deliver the course.

- ❑ Create content, or use existing content, specific to the association.

- ❑ Establish a map to organize course elements.

- ❑ Develop and test the course.

❏ Determine the appropriate method of delivery, such as synchronous (live), asynchronous (self-paced), or a combination of both.

❏ Determine who will deliver the course, if the course is instructor led, and provide training/instruction on how best to conduct online training.

❏ Compile a final internal course outline, including content separated by session and participant time required per session.

❏ Notify participants of program specifics, including course name, course URL, start date, session dates and times, access information (such as user name/password), and support information (including what they can expect and how to get help).

❏ Deliver course session(s) to participants on schedule, and complete on schedule.

❏ Encourage participants to communicate with the instructor and remind them about how to get technical support.

❏ Conduct a post-course test via an online form.

❏ Conduct a post-course evaluation via an online form.

❏ Use post-course measurement techniques to determine the achievement of learning objectives and overall course goals.

AAMSE Strategic Planning Course Results

A course evaluation was conducted following the second and final session of the AAMSE online course via an online form. Responses from all 15 participants were evaluated to determine if the course objectives and the overall goal of creating a model for placing association education programs online using the latest in Internet technology were achieved.

Evaluation questions were designed in the following categories: the effectiveness of the instructor, course content, areas of difficulty, areas of strength, and overall experience. Note that the level of participant topic knowledge at the start of the course was very high. Using a selection of yes or no, multiple-choice, and open-ended questions, responses from participants included:

Instructor

- The course instructor received perfect marks for her level of knowledge, interactivity with participants, and level of enthusiasm.

Course Content

- 70 percent of the respondents felt that the content was related to the association industry.
- 62 percent of the respondents strongly agreed that the content was relevant to association goals.

Areas of Strength

- "The reading and course material was extremely helpful and informative."
- "General overview provided was helpful prior to starting."
- "The material was really excellent. The online chat was easy to use."
- "The subject and instructor were areas of strength that helped the course."
- "The interactive forms and tests helped to reinforce learning."
- "The opportunity for interaction. Learning from others will be beneficial to my organization."

Areas of Difficulty

- "Reading materials online, suggest printing and reading, or sending pre-reading material to participants ahead of time."
- "Had to load the most up-to-date browser to participate."
- "Difficulty getting into and using Webboard for group discussion, suggest practicing prior to logging in to discussion."
- "Delays with logging into and receiving messages during Chat, possibly due to my slow computer."
- "Using AOL to participate, including not being able to receive attachments with instructions, slow load times with advanced application."
- "Time to get into the course on successive visits. Suggest saving log-ins and passwords to make re-entry quicker."

Overall Experience

- 75 percent of respondents felt that the online course was moderately to very effective.

Additional Comments

- "Great experience and a good way to learn how online education can work."
- "Do things the most efficient way possible and be customer-driven."
- "Participation was very useful for me. This, finally, seems like a viable alternative to traveling to meetings, and much less

expensive. This format makes it much easier to network, which is almost mandatory today."

- "Need to be very careful to make education convenient, and for the delivery to enhance the subject."

- "Reading and direction from leaders was excellent."

- "Going through this course will help me design a strategic planning 'blue print' which can be implemented with each group as they continue to grow."

Based on evaluation responses, follow-up discussions with participants, and the fact that participants began the course with a high level of knowledge on the subject of association strategic planning, the AAMSE online course achieved both target objectives and the overall goal.

Summary

As organizations transition from classroom learning to instructor-facilitated online learning, the challenge of taking passive, dependent students and turning them into independent students needs to be considered. Traditional instructor-led training is passive and depends on the instructor for knowledge transfer. One of the early lessons learned is that with online education, it cannot be assumed that because training is self-directed, the passive, dependent students will become assertive and independent. Therefore, a solid online education strategy should consider how the prospective student prefers to learn and the level of involvement by the course instructor.

With the online education market still in its infancy, a majority of students are still more comfortable with a traditional learning environment. This is important to remember in order to concentrate on the user-centered learning portion of an online course first, before the technology. By focusing on the learning portion first, the instructor can help students become more comfortable with the online education environment, which will help lead to the achievement of the learning objectives.

Instructors are quickly learning that to properly facilitate online education courses, students must perceive that the instructors are always available, much as in a traditional environment. The simulation of constant availability is achieved through various methods, including virtual office hours, e-mail, discussion groups, and chat forums. These technologies allow students to become more comfortable with the environment and help the instructor because they are scheduled for the most part.

The instructor for the AAMSE online course in this study, Ginger Nichols, applied her considerable traditional classroom training experience to online training. Nichols focused her experience on the learning portion of the course and made herself available via multiple methods of communication to help increase the students' comfort level. Nichols' approach to instruction was key to the success of this model.

The feedback of the AAMSE online course participants, response from members of the executive panel, and benchmarking conducted throughout this study indicate that this association online education model is a viable model you can apply to your own organization's online education strategy. Because this model is built on a framework of solid training principles integrated with newly forming technologies, it has the added value of flexibility and adaptability.

6. Vision for the Future

The opportunity for associations to deliver online education is here. Dramatic increases in the number of users connected through the Internet, power of the desktop computer, and bandwidth to deliver interactivity, along with the need for knowledge-based solutions have created an overnight industry.

As technologies develop, online education will evolve. It is important for associations to begin building Web sites today that feature scalable architecture and cross-platform capability, so that they will be able to add future technologies without having to entirely redesign sites. In the next few years, more educational events will be conducted over the Web. Associations should actively seek out experience and member support during this period and should be poised to take advantage of new technologies as they become affordable, effective, and relevant.

Using emerging technologies and user-centered design, educational Web sites of tomorrow will emphasize community development in addition to knowledge transfer. Students will learn from asynchronous modules, from instructors in synchronous sessions, and from each other. They will dynamically add to the content of the educational event through chat sessions, threaded discussions, and broadcast homework assignments. Educational games and process simulations will present active learning scenarios to students in increasingly engaging formats. Instructors will help students in collaborative work sessions, and instructors will help select which student responses should be broadcast on the Web to add to the course content.

Synchronous and asynchronous events will co-mingle within content areas, and the students' level of interaction will increase. Animation, video, audio, and database-intensive applications will be more common as user bandwidth increases and technologies improve. Associations that build a sense of community, maintain current content, provide consistent course pricing models, apply and monitor management systems, and incorporate effective technologies on their education Web sites will put themselves in the best position to compete for the attention of potential students.

Increased competition is on the horizon. For-profits, universities, and associations that have developed successful online education models will soon realize that they can reach out to new markets and perhaps even redefine the meaning of membership. The competition can easily come from a company in an entirely different field or from one that doesn't yet exist. Associations, however, are in the best position to capitalize on this convergence because they have the market, content, expertise, and community to leverage. Associations that deploy a technology business plan that includes online education will improve their member benefits and position by leveraging existing strengths.

Associations are challenged to move effectively and quickly to maximize the opportunity and minimize competition. Each association will need to customize its approach based on its membership, environment, and where it is in its life cycle. Some may partner with for-profit organizations while others may start with customized but low-level interactive programs developed by the association. Still others may choose to develop high-end interactive models of online education. You will need to decide which is the right approach to take for your association, how to migrate education offerings to the Web to fully capitalize on this growing opportunity, and what your own business plan or roadmap to the future is.

To be a viable force in the future, associations will need to:

- Have a strong grasp of the technologies and programming that are currently available (see chapter 2).

- Learn how other associations have moved toward an online education offering (see chapters 3 and 4).

- Assess the most appropriate model for their members given members' technical and behavioral readiness and the association's financial resources by applying the process checklist and operational and executive tips in chapter 5.

- Determine what tools are necessary and if the course should be developed inside or outside the organization (see chapters 2, 3, and 4).

- Understand the potential for interactivity and what they and their members need to prepare for by studying the model described in chapter 5.

The opportunity is enormous, the technical and human obstacles are disappearing, and the time to leverage your association's brand is now!

Appendix A: Methodology

The initial steps of this study included determining existing use of online education within associations, identifying issues association executives felt were critical to developing successful online education, and identifying potential case study participants. In January 1998, a survey to support this study was adapted from a Fusion Productions corporate study and administered online. A letter was sent to 2,834 association executives asking them to respond to the online survey, resulting in 444 completed and usable responses.

At the same time the survey was being conducted, environmental scans were conducted from March 1, 1998, to July 15, 1998 to identify where organizations might be in their evolution toward online education and to see what could be learned from their current activities. Researchers did the following:

- Conducted in-depth case study interviews with five associations:
  - Special Libraries Association, Washington, D.C.;
  - Association of Public Safety Communications Officials International, South Daytona, Fla.;
  - American College of Healthcare Executives, Chicago;
  - American Association for Clinical Chemistry, Inc., Washington, D.C.; and
  - Association of Public Health Laboratories, Washington, D.C.

- Conducted interviews with 29 associations, thus generating best practices from executives and operational managers.

- Interviewed leading industry advisers from the IBT Group, Falls Church, Va.; the MASIE Center, Saratoga Springs, N.Y.; the Computer Education Management Association, Los Gatos, Calif.; and the American Society for Training and Development, Alexandria, Va.

- Reviewed corporate online endeavors by Hewlett Packard, Palo Alto, Calif.; Dow Chemical, Midland, Mich.; and AutoDesk, San Rafael, Calif.

- Reviewed 30 online education tool vendors, including Allen Communications, Salt Lake City, Utah; Avilar Technologies, Laurel, Md.; Mentorware, Santa Clara, Calif.; and Avalon Information Technologies, Brampton, Ontario, Canada.

- Reviewed 51 university online endeavors and interviewed representatives of the University of Phoenix, University of California at Los Angeles, and the State University of New York.

- Participated in an online course delivered by PACE University, White Plains, N.Y., and managed by the Special Libraries Association.

- Reviewed articles and white papers by industry experts, leading universities, and online education tool vendors.

Recognizing that most associations are not in the position to "experiment" with a high-end online education program, an association online course was designed and delivered. This online course used Fusion Productions' Web programming and servers, software from technology partners (Cyberrealm and Allen Communications), and selected members of the American Association of Medical Society Executives (AAMSE), Chicago. The course instructor, Ginger Nichols, president of GinCommGroup, San Francisco, was selected based on both her skill with the subject matter and her knowledge of associations. Nichols donated her time, content, and objectives for the online course on a one-time basis.

Using a well-tested and proprietary survey, AAMSE conducted an association-wide technology and education survey. The objective was to identify candidates with the necessary technical capability to participate in an online education course. From this initial survey, 70 members qualified for the online course. To control the course quality, 20 students were selected from those who qualified, with 15 participating based on time and travel constraints.

The overall goal with designing and delivering an online course was to create an innovative model for placing association education programs online using the latest in Internet technology. From this endeavor the ASAE Foundation would be able to provide tips and issues of which associations attempting such a project should be aware.

To ensure that a product would be developed that addresses the needs of a diverse group of associations, a six-member association executive panel was established. The panel's role was to review work processes and output and provide feedback, identify potential association models to review, and provide input on the new model created. The association executive panel included:

- Robin Kriegel, CAE, executive director of the American Association of Medical Society Executives

- Kathie Berry, CAE, vice president of finance and administration for Associated Builders and Contractors, Rosslyn, Va.

- Jeri A. Semer, CAE, executive director of the Association for Telecommunications Professionals in Higher Education, Lexington, Ky.

- Joan Campbell, CAE, executive vice president of the Home Sewing Association, New York

- Dave Fellers, CAE, executive director of the American Society of Plastic and Reconstructive Surgeons, Arlington Heights, Ill.

- Bryan Silbermann, CAE, president of the Produce Marketing Association, Newark, Del.

Appendix B: Software Vendor Fact Reports

Allen Communication

5 Triad Center, Fifth Floor
Salt Lake City, UT 84180
Phone: (800) 325-7850
          (801) 537-7800
Fax: (801) 537-7805 (main)
          (801) 799-7378 (sales)
URL: www.Allencomm.com

- Complete
- Analysis
- Design
- Development
- Evaluation
- Management
- Synchronous
- Asynchronous

Since 1981 Allen Communication has provided multimedia training solutions to trainers and developers worldwide. Allen offers a full range of solutions, including software tools, full-service custom development, hands-on training, and critical point consulting.

Designer's Edge is a preauthoring tool that assists in creating storyboards and lesson plans broken into 12 phases and associated tasks to guide you through the process. Net Synergy, added to Designer's Edge, allows you to output Designer's Edge storyboards directly to HTML and JAVA, allowing for immediate Web training availability.

> **System:** • analysis • design • development • evaluation
>
> **Benefits:** Links hundreds of prebuilt templates to specific instructional strategies; customizable interface; step-by-step guidance and context-sensitive help.
>
> **System Requirements:** PC compatible running Windows 95 or Windows NT (4.0 or higher); minimum Pentium 90 processor (Pentium 133 recommended); minimum 32 meg RAM (64 or higher recommended); SVGA graphics card.
>
> **Price:** Call for price.

Quest provides a dynamic, visual authoring environment for both novice and expert training developers. Its object-oriented environment allows you to create highly interactive courses quickly, without any programming. It is easy to use and flexible.

> **System:** • design   • development
>
> **Benefits:** Simplifies the creation and delivery process for online learning; built-in CMI capabilities help track return on invest-

ment; ActiveX support makes it easy to embed just-in-time training into third-party documents.

System Requirements: PC compatible running a Windows 3.x application; minimum Pentium 90 processor (Pentium 133 recommended); minimum 32 meg RAM (64 or higher recommended); SVGA graphics card.

Price: Call for price.

Manager's Edge is a dynamic management shell that allows students to control the presentation of assigned course activities, and allows training managers and administrators to manage the delivery of all kinds of training—from multi-media lessons to stand-up lectures.

System: • management

Benefits: Organizes courses in a natural hierarchy to clarify relationships between key topics and activities; collects and merges data from various sources to a central location; combines various types of training into a unified curriculum, including online and offline activities; adapts training delivery to specific user needs, such as language preference, job function, performance level, etc.

System Requirements: PC compatible running Windows 95 or Windows NT (4.0 or higher); minimum Pentium 90 processor (Pentium 133 recommended); minimum 32 meg RAM (64 or higher recommended); SVGA graphics card.

Price: Call for price.

Avalon Information Technologies, Inc.
Caroline Cheung, Manager, Product Applications
1 Kenview Boulevard
Brampton, Ontario L6T 5E6, Canada
Phone:　(905) 792-2072
Fax:　　 (905) 702-2594
E-mail:　ccheung@atlantis.com
URL:　　 www.atlantis.com/avalon

- Complete
- Analysis
- Design
- Development
- Evaluation
- Management
- Synchronous
- Asynchronous

Avalon Information Technologies develops interactive multimedia systems, distance-learning products, and performance support tools. Avalon's products combine advanced technology with innovative engineering to meet today's need for the timely, cost-effective delivery of information and distance learning.

BRIGHTLight 2.0 is a unique, low-bandwidth multimedia distance-learning system that combines remote, instructor-led course delivery with integrated performance support and information features.

> **System:** • design • development • evaluation • management

> **Benefits:** Offers an economical, effective solution by bringing training to each learner's workplace, where it becomes an integral part of the job and can be applied right away.

> **System Requirements:** For Windows 95 or Windows NT. Instructor station: Pentium PC, 100MHz or faster, graphics card supporting 800x600 resolution and 256 colors or higher, SVGA monitor, minimum 16 megs RAM (32 megs recommended), Windows compatible sound card, 4x CD-ROM, 28.8K modem or network adapter, 16 megs free hard disk space. Student station: Pentium PC, 75 MHz or faster, graphics card supporting 800x600 resolution and 256 colors or higher, SVGA monitor, minimum 16 megs RAM, Windows compatible sound card, 4x CD-ROM, 14.4K modem or network adapter, 16 megs free hard disk space.

> **Price:** Standard prices: 1–10 units/seats = $995 per unit/seat; 11–25 units/seats = $795 per unit/seat; 26–100 units/seats = $495 per unit/seat; 101–500 units/seats = $395 per unit/seat; 501–1,000 units/seats = $295 per unit/seat; 1,000+ units/seats = $195 per unit/seat. Call for pricing on site licensing.

Avilar Technologies, Inc.
Jerry Horsewood, President
8750-9 Cherry Lane
Laurel, MD 20707-6208
Phone: (301) 725-7014
Fax: (301) 725-0980
URL: www.avilar.com

- Complete
- Analysis
- Design
- Development
- Evaluation
- Management
- Asynchronous

Avilar Technologies, Inc., affiliated with AdaSoft, Inc., has 14 years of successful business history. The partners have completed many complex development projects for the Department of Defense and applied physics labs.

WebMentor is a comprehensive software system for easy development and management of courses using the Internet. WebMentor includes authoring for nonprogrammers, assessment testing, student records, enrollment, registration, e-commerce, and collaboration for delivery to a browser over the Internet.

System: • complete • asynchronous

Benefits: Authoring or course development for nontechnical trainers; turnkey solution that automates delivery and administration; allows collaborative learning through the Internet or intranet using e-mail, bulletin boards, forums, and discussion groups; supports the roles of author, editor, publisher, and administrator.

System Requirements: Windows NT (Enterprise server); Windows 95 and Windows NT (authoring); Netscape Navigator 3.0 or higher; Internet Explorer 3.0 or higher; Microsoft Access or Microsoft SQL; NT server and either Microsoft or Netscape.

Price: Based on total number of registrations: 10 = $3,000; 30 = $5,000; 100 = $8,000; 1,000 = $14,000; 10,000 = $20,000. As students complete the course, there is room for new student registrations.

Mentorware, Inc.
Naresh Bala, Vice President, Sales & Marketing
4701 Patrick Henry Drive, Suite 1101
Santa Clara, CA 95054-1893
Phone: (408) 566-8800, ext. 202
Fax: (408) 566-8808
E-mail: naresh@mentorware.com
URL: www.mentorware.com

• Complete
• Analysis
• Design
• Development
• Evaluation
• Management
• Synchronous
• Asynchronous

Mentorware builds a product that allows organizations to build training content and deploy it over the Web. It has been used in a number of Fortune 500 companies to improve their operational efficiency—primarily by streamlining training of their employees who deal with customers. Some of the content built internally include products, policies, and procedures training material for sales executives, contract employees, HR professionals, and customer support.

Mentorware is an intuitive paradigm for training, integrating the development, delivery, and administration functions. Mentorware provides an extensive and flexible reporting structure that facilitates relevant feedback to content developers and students through detailed statistics and results on tests and questions; total control over authorization of classes and users through a combination of password protection and integration with encryption technologies; integrated training systems with other enterprise systems, such as LDAP, PeopleSoft, Sales Automation Systems, etc.; an open format, template-oriented, and team approach to course development.

System: • complete

Benefits: Extensive experience with helping organizations improve their efficiency through use of the Web for on-demand training, helping clients achieve an averge 15% to 20% increase in the efficiency of their support and sales staff and new hires into the company.

System Requirements: Windows NT, UNIX, Sun Solaris, Oracle; Netscape Navigator 3.0 or higher; Internet Explorer 3.0 or higher.

Price: Call for price.

NOTES

- **Complete** system incorporates all or most of the following principles as an end-to-end system for designing and delivering online education.
- **Analysis** involves conducting a needs assessment; specifying content and objectives; selecting delivery systems; establishing educational goals; planning evaluation strategies.
- **Design** involves creating graphic treatment specifications; specifying instructional interactions; using a flow chart program; creating a prototype; writing script; conducting formative reviews.
- **Development** involves creating the course; creating graphics; preparing study materials; integrating optical media with content.
- **Evaluation** involves testing/validating elements developed; conducting participant testing; conducting impact evaluation.
- **Management** involves managing program registration; managing prerequisites; data handling; reporting; developing learning profiles.

Appendix C: Full-Line Software Vendors and Applications

A full-line software vendor creates a tool or group of tools that is designed to facilitate most or all of an organization's online training objectives. The following vendors represent a small, illustrative sampling of full-line tool developers.

Asymetrix Learning Systems, Inc.

www.asymetrix.com

ToolBook II Assistant helps author and deliver training and online learning lessons quickly, easily, and economically via the Internet, an intranet, a local area network, or CD-ROM. Assistant uses an intuitive drag-and-drop interface to make the authoring process more efficient.

Docent, Inc.

www.docent.com

Docent Enterprise is an enterprise training system designed to complement business objectives by supporting each phase of development, including needs assessment, course creation, delivery, management, and results tracking. Based on open standards, Enterprise can be customized to meet unique requirements and processes, while maintaining security and confidentiality.

KnowledgeSoft, Inc.

www.knowledgesoft.com

KoTrain allows organizations to assemble courses and convert content, administer and manage training, and assess and validate learning. KoTrain uses templates and wizards that help developers create courses, online advertisements, quizzes and tests, and basic performance objectives. KoTrain offers a unique "adaptive" assessment method. Using a model that applies complex algorithms to analyze correct and incorrect answers, KoTrain measures skill proficiency to a selected degree of confidence. Once the model determines statistically that a learner does or does not possess a skill, questioning ends, maximizing the efficiency of the assessment.

Lotus Development

www.lotus.com

LearningSpace brings together organizational content with technology elements, including live, asynchronous, and self-paced delivery. LearningSpace helps create live, virtual classrooms and asynchronous, instructor-facilitated courses and adds structure, tracking, and maintenance capabilities to self-paced materials.

Macromedia

www.macromedia.com

Authorware Attain is an authoring tool for creating online learning applications. Authorware allows training developers, instructional designers, and subject matter experts to develop learning applications and deploy them across the Web, local area networks, and CD-ROM. Authorware is part of a family of products within Macromedia's Enterprise Learning System of integrated, open, scalable, learning tools and technologies.

WBT Systems

www.wbtsystems.com

TopClass Creator allows for the rapid assembly of online courses by combining any Web-compatible content into learning modules. Creator is designed for content experts and simplifies the process through open integration with popular tools like Microsoft Office and FrontPage. Creator also offers the flexibility to incorporate advanced Web applications and streaming media. Other features include visual course creation, reusable learning modules, dynamic course content modification, controlled access to content, and comprehensive assessment supporting 20 question types. Creator is part of a comprehensive family of products that can be used to facilitate online education.

A specialized software vendor creates a tool or group of tools that is designed to facilitate specific aspects of an organization's online education program. The following vendors represent a small, illustrative sampling of specialized tool developers.

Centra Software, Inc.

www.centra.com

Symposium is a content delivery system that provides an interface for advanced integrated multiway audio conferencing, interactive and instant yes/no responses and feedback, live application sharing, whiteboard, breakout rooms and labs, just-in-time content updates, multicast option, text chat, control hand-off to co-presenters, spontaneous polling, and evaluation tools. This product is good for highly interactive team collaboration, workshops, and hands-on training and supports up to 250 simultaneous users per event in a live, structured environment.

Contigo Software

www.contigo.com

Contigo Internet Conferencing System (ICS) is a virtual conferencing system with a feature set that addresses all phases of the presentation process, for true "anywhere, anytime, anyone" implementation. ICS incorporates pre-, during, and post-event system attributes that collectively make ICS accessible to remote and nontechnical personnel, nonintrusive to internal information technology departments, and convenient to audiences spanning virtually unlimited geographic areas.

DataBeam

www.databeam.com

neT.120 Conference Server is a software product that enables users on any platform equipped with an HTML browser to participate in multipoint data conferences on any network, sharing documents, images, and applications. Available add-on tools help facilitate audio and video conferencing.

Gyrus Systems, Inc.

www.gyrus.com

Training Wizard 98 is a comprehensive training management program that integrates registration, scheduling, tracking, budgeting, and reporting functions for managers responsible for organizational training. Features include advanced reporting, easy use, course grouping, automation of repetitive tasks, compatibility with a wide range of popular databases, and the ability to place a course catalog online.

Interactive Learning International Corporation

www.ilinc.com

LearnLinc is a real-time content delivery system enabled by popular online technology to deliver live, instructor-led training to employees or students via the Internet, corporate or university intranet, or wide area network. LearnLinc specializes in recreating the interactive classroom environment by simultaneously connecting to students via the PC using audio or video conferencing; synchronizing multimedia content and software applications on student computers; recognizing student class participation; enabling students to singularly address the class; and incorporating question and answer, text chat, and video streaming.

Question Mark Corporation

www.questionmark.com

Question Mark Perception provides for the creation and delivery of tests, quizzes, and surveys on intranets or the Internet. Begin by authoring questions using templates in a Windows 95/NT environment, then store them on a Web server. Participants can then log in, with a user name and password if desired, to take a test or respond to a survey. The questions are delivered, in order or randomly, with standard Internet browsers and include feedback and scoring.

The Saratoga Group

www.saratogagroup.com/home.htm

CyberWISE Online is a training management system for the intranet and Internet. It can be used to centrally manage and deliver training in any format, including computer-based training, Web-based training, multimedia, video, text-based, or live classroom instruction. CyberWISE Online helps to create a catalog of courses, provides online testing, and provides online registration for classes.

Appendix E: Online Education Service Vendors

The following four vendors represent organizations that provide in-depth online education services. These companies service the online education needs of those organizations seeking to develop an approach method A program, such as purchasing the ability to use an existing online course under a private label name.

DigitalThink

www.digitalthink.com

DigitalThink delivers training via the Web to companies and individuals on computer science, multimedia tools, the Internet, and other topics. It has two missions: (1) to assist companies in training their customers and employees, and (2) to enable consumers to conveniently learn what they want, when they want.

DigitalThink works to build an online community of students, tutors, and instructors by being more interactive than traditional methods of learning. An example of this interactivity is its use of tutors to answer individual e-mail messages and engage in threaded discussions and chat sessions. It enhances this community with exclusive agreements with best-selling authors and topic experts to create original content just for the Web.

Web-based courses are sold directly from its Web site, or as blocks of seats directly to training departments. Course prices range from $125 to $450 per student.

GartnerGroup Learning

www.gartner.com

GartnerGroup Learning is a technology-based software education developer that provides information technology professionals and end users with technology-based training products in multiple delivery formats. These formats include computer-based training, multimedia CD-ROM, video, and the Internet. GartnerGroup Learning has also formed relationships with Microsoft, Novell, Oracle, and Sylvan Prometric to provide content, delivery formats, and certification.

GartnerGroup provides technology-based, self-directed learning to help accommodate the skill levels of all students. Its customers determine the comprehensive curriculum needed, and it offers a multiformat approach to training that allows a client to pick and choose the delivery format or combination of formats that best suits its needs.

UOL Publishing, Inc.

www.uol.com/webuol/index.cfm

UOL Publishing, Inc., publishes interactive, Web-based courseware delivered through the Internet or corporate intranets. UOL offers what it calls full-service solutions, including more than 350 courses in management, computer applications, business, technical skills, and more.

UOL provides a variety of services, including custom courseware development, Web-based certification and testing, instructor training, CD-ROM, custom print-based courseware development, publishing, distribution, and course customization based on the needs of the client.

Ziff Davis University

www.zdu.com

Ziff Davis University (ZDU) offers a unique method of online learning by making its course listing more attainable to anyone. It allows people to take any of its courses and pay monthly or annually. This allows freedom and flexibility to take as many courses as you want and explore topics you may not have otherwise considered taking due to prohibitive costs. ZDU offers a wide range of computer classes for $7.95 a month or $69.95 a year. Courses are taught by industry experts, book authors, and professional trainers. In addition, ZDU offers continuing education credits and has its own certificates for completion.

Resources

Articles/Reports

- Allen Communication; Training Fast Tracks newsletter series www.allencomm.com/about/fasttracks.html

- The MASIE Center—www.masie.com/list and www.masie.com/articles/cbt.html

E-mail List

- Bluesquirrel News—www.bluesquirrel.com

- Emerging Trends—www.emergeonline.com

- ServiceScan—www.servicescan.com

Web Links

- Enabling Technologies—www.online.uillinois.edu/links/enabling_tech.html

Web Sites

- Fusion Productions—www.fusionproductions.com

- Microsoft OLL Center—www.microsoft.com/train_cert/OLIC

- Tilt Technology in learning and teaching—www.at.nwu.edu/ltg/training/tilt

White Papers

- Brandon Hall—www.multimediatraining.com/faq.html

- Docent—www.docent.com/solutions/whtpapers/index.htm

- Fusion Productions—The Networked Association

- University of South Florida—http://itech1.coe.uga.edu/itforum/paper26/paper26.html

- UOL Publishing—www.uol.com/website/benefits.htm

Glossary

Asynchronous communication—Self-directed or self-paced delivery, generally an ongoing discussion between two or more people online with no geographic or time limitations. Popular methods of communicating include e-mail and established discussion boards.

Authentication—A technique by which access to Internet or intranet resources requires the user to identify himself or herself by entering a user name and password.

Bandwidth—The maximum speed at which data can be transmitted between computers in a network.

Browser—A software application that displays documents delivered from network servers. Browsers vary by vendor and may support text-based information, graphics-based information, or both. Examples include Internet Explorer and Netscape Navigator.

CD-ROM—A format and system for retrieving, storing, and recording electronic information on a compact disc that is read using an optical drive.

Chat forum—The ability for members, staff, suppliers, and others to interact in real-time using any Java-enabled browser and promote dynamic exchange of information and community building.

Community—Closely correlates to a real-world organization on the Internet, where users can find out the latest news, chat with friends and colleagues, discuss current issues, and more.

Computer-based training (CBT)—Instruction delivered to students via a specific computer application. CD-ROM is the most popular method of delivering CBT.

Cookies—Small text files (usually less than 1k in size) that your browser picks up at many Web sites and stores on your hard drive. Generated from information supplied by the user, they help to personalize content delivery on subsequent visits.

Discussion board—An online area where people can post and reply to questions and comments.

Distance learning—The delivery of instruction via multimedia computers, satellite, and/or teleconferencing, where the teacher is in one place and the students in another.

Domain name—The unique name that identifies an Internet site. Domain names always have two or more parts, separated by a dot. The part on the left is the most specific, and the part on the right is the most general. A given server may have more than one domain name but a given domain name points to only one server.

Electronic commerce—Business that takes place between parties, one the supplier and the other the customer, transmitting inquiries, orders, invoices, payments, etc., directly through their computer systems.

Electronic mail (e-mail)—The exchange of messages through computers.

FAQ—A file that contains frequently asked questions and answers.

File transfer protocol (FTP)—A standard for moving files from one computer to another. A computer on the Internet that specifically stores files for users to transfer to their own computers is called an FTP site.

Form—An HTML page that allows the user to input information, which then passes this information back to the server.

Home page—The main page of a Web site. The home page provides visitors with an overview and links to the rest of the site. It often contains or links to a table of contents for the site.

Hyper text markup language (HTML)—The text-based language used to construct Web pages and is interpreted by Web browsers.

Hyper text transfer protocol (HTTP)—A standard method of transferring data between a Web server and a Web browser.

Instructional systems design (ISD)—A formal process for designing traditional instructor-led or computer-based training.

Internet—An international computer network that connects government, academic, and business institutions.

Intranet—Any network contained within an organization; used primarily with reference to networks using Internet technology.

Java—A modern programming language used to bring Web pages to life. Java programs are referred to as applets. One significant benefit of Java is that a Java program can run on many different types of computers.

JavaScript—A programming language for developing advanced interactivity into programs. The Web browser interprets JavaScript statements embedded in an HTML page.

Knowledge management—Organizational processes that seek a synergistic combination of data- and information-processing capacity, using information technologies and the innovative capacity of human beings.

Multimedia—A computer application that uses more than one media, including text, graphics, animations, audio, and video. CBT and WBT programs are often referred to as multimedia because they tend to incorporate more than one medium in their design.

Platform—The operating system (i.e., Windows 95, Windows NT, etc.) that is used to turn on a computer.

Process simulation—A training method used online to show the visitor step-by-step actions for completing a process or procedure. This can be displayed in graphics form, with video growing in popularity.

Protocol—A standard process; a set of rules and conditions that perform a particular function. Examples include:

- File transfer protocol (FTP)
- Internet protocol (IP) address
- Transmission control protocol/internet protocol (TCP/IP)
- Post office protocol (POP)

Scalable—Hardware or software that can be expanded as required in the future. For instance, a particular application may be set up to run for two concurrent users but can be scaled up for more users if the organization needs to expand in the future.

Scripts—A program consisting of a series of instructions. Scripts are often run when an application program is started. They are written in a specific programming language.

Server—A server distributes the processing of a computer application between two computers, the client and the server—the goal being to exploit the power of each. The client is normally a PC. The application program will access data and perform processing on the server and, using the data obtained via the server, more processing tasks will be performed on the client. The application can be used by more than one user.

Streaming media—Real-time audio and video delivered via the Internet to educate, entertain, or inform. The selected medium is "streamed" to end users, allowing them to view or listen to it before it is completely downloaded to their system.

Synchronous communication—"Live" online communication (instructor facilitated), including chat, shared whiteboards, voice-based teleconferencing, and videoconferencing.

Teleconference—The instantaneous exchange of audio, video, or text between two or more individuals or groups in different locations. Each person is recorded on a camera, and the image is played back on the other participants' PCs by a special application program.

Universal resource locator (URL)—A means of identifying an exact location of a document or Web site on the Internet. A URL is inserted in a document in the following format: scheme://host-domain[:port]/path/filename.

Videoconference—See Teleconference.

Web-based training (WBT)—Instruction delivered to students over the Internet or an intranet and displayed with a Web browser. WBT is most often on-demand training stored on a server, accessed across a network, and administered by the training provider.

Whiteboard—An application program that permits several users linked via a network to update the same physical document—just as if they were all in a room together gathered around a whiteboard.

World Wide Web—All of the resources and users on the Internet that use hypertext transport protocol, a set of rules for exchanging files.

The Authors

Fusion Productions is a meeting and Internet design and technology company with 22 years of experience in providing associations with meeting production, learning, and technology services. Technology services include surveys and consulting, Web strategy and design, and online integration of conventions, tradeshows, and education.

Fusion has over 300 meeting and technology clients, including the American Speech–Language Hearing Association, PricewaterhouseCoopers, Aircraft Owners and Pilots Association (AOPA), Eastman Kodak Company, Bausch & Lomb, Meeting Professionals International (MPI), Sun Microsystems, and Xplor International. Fusion staff researched and wrote the ASAE Foundation's World-Class Web Sites (1998).

Don Dea is co-founder of Fusion Productions. Dea's professional experience includes 10 years of leadership and a position as chairman of the board for the Association for the Blind and Visually Impaired for Greater Rochester and Monroe County. He also has had 15 years of sales, marketing, and executive management experience, including five years as general manager of U.S. Channel Operations for Xerox Corporation. Dea also has launched a personal computer company that reached $90 million in sales within a 36-month period. His association technology experience includes:

- Three-time producer of ASAE's technology conference and
- Producer of several association events deploying Web-based technology capabilities for several organizations, including:
  - Society of Cardiovascular & Interventional Radiology
  - Meeting Professionals International
  - Sun Microsystems

Dea is also a recognized association, Internet, meetings, and technology authority. Most recently, he has spoken at ASAE's Technology Conference on best association Web sites and best practices. He serves as a speaker/consultant for MPI, AOPA, International Association of Emergency Managers, and American Association of

Medical Society Executives on best practices in managing association Web sites. Dea served as Xerox's representative in the president's Executive Exchange Program as a special assistant to the Attorney General, Department of Justice. Dea is a graduate of the Senior Executive program, Sloan School of Management, Massachusetts Institute of Technology.

Hugh K. Lee, president of Fusion Productions, is a past board member for ASAE, New York Society of Association Executives, and MPI. He designed and implemented ASAE's 1995 Association Technology Trends Survey and the Web-related section added to the 1997 Association Technology Trends Study. A recognized speaker, author, and consultant to associations, Lee is an ASAE Associate Fellow and has also received both ASAE's Distinguished Contributions Award and MPI's Industry Award.

You can reach both Don Dea and Hugh K. Lee:

- Through their Web site: http://www.fusionproductions.com
- By fax: (716) 872-2014
- By phone: (800) 828-6306

You may visit Fusion Productions' Web site to review archived progress of both the 1997 ASAE Foundation Study (World-Class Web Sites) and this 1998 study and to learn more about advanced Internet applications.

The Contributors

Industry Advisers

Anne Blouin, CAE, Director of Education, the American Society for Training and Development. The American Society for Training and Development (ASTD) is the world's premier professional association in the field of workplace learning and performance. Founded in 1944, ASTD represents more than 70,000 members in the field of workplace learning and performance, who come from every area of the growing industry and from more than 150 countries across the globe. ASTD's leadership and members work in multinational corporations, small- and medium-sized businesses, government agencies, colleges, and universities.

To assist both members and nonmembers with their professional development, ASTD convenes a number of specialized events throughout the year, each of which brings together leading industry professionals. ASTD also provides myriad valuable products and services. And as one of the largest publishers in training, learning, and performance, ASTD offers a wide selection of periodicals, books, newslettors, research reports, and videotapes.

Philippe S. Clarke, President and CEO, IBT Group. IBT Group helps organizations build learning communities and transfer knowledge and skills to their employees, members, partners, and customers. IBT Group accomplishes this transfer through training, online eventcasting, video capture, and consulting services. It custom builds training products to the specifications of each customer; products range from CD-ROM to intranet- and Internet-based modules. Its eventcasting services enable organizations to broadcast conferences, meetings, sales presentations, or other events on the Internet and keep them available there for 12 months or more. IBT Group's consulting services help organizations determine the needs of their employees, members, partners, and customers. IBT Group conducts analyses to determine training needs as well as to describe the effects of the current organizational culture. They provide recommendations for meeting those training needs and shifting the culture to improve its effectiveness.

Wayne Hodgins, Board President, the Computer Education Management Association. The Computer Education Management

Association (CEdMA) provides a forum for managers and directors of computer education organizations to discuss issues in computer training. CEdMA's goal is to work as an organization to shape the future of the industry for excellence in education, training, and learning in ways that benefit members, customers, partners, and employees within member organizations.

Working in fast-paced, dynamic technical environments brings major challenges and satisfaction to the managers of corporate training organizations. CEdMA's success is the ability to share experiences, successes, and even not-so-successful endeavors. Founded in 1991, CEdMA is a unique professional association made up of individuals who manage training businesses in companies manufacturing hardware and software products.

Elliott Masie, President, the MASIE Center. The MASIE Center is an international think-tank located in Saratoga Springs, N.Y. The Center is dedicated to exploring the intersection of learning and technology and is focused on these key areas:

- How people learn to use technology
- How technology can be used to help people learn
- New models for providing learning across distance and time
- New roles for training and learning professionals

The MASIE Center provides its services to major corporations and technology providers throughout the world. The Center provides research, perspectives, training, learning products, and consulting on these key issues. The MASIE Center was formed to provide a clear-thinking leadership hub for the next generation of learning and technology solutions.

Executive Panel and Faculty

Kathie Berry, CAE, CPA, is vice president of finance and administration for Associated Builders and Contractors (ABC), a national trade association representing 20,000 members in 83 chapters throughout the country. ABC and its affiliates have a staff of 75 in Rosslyn, Va. Berry oversees the finance, information systems, human resources, and facilities management areas of ABC. She is an ASAE Fellow and has served as chairman of ASAE's Finance and Administration Section Council. She has been active in ASAE and the Greater Washington Society of Association Executives and has been a frequent presenter at programs for both organizations. She is a graduate of Mary Washington College.

Joan Campbell, CAE, is executive vice president of the Home Sewing Association, a trade association representing suppliers, retailers, and educators in the home sewing industry. Her experience in the field of association management spans over 24 years. Upon graduation from Michigan State University, she began her career at the Michigan Hospital Association. Before moving to Chicago in 1985, she also held positions as a lobbyist with two trade associations in Michigan. While in Chicago, Campbell worked for Haeger & Associates, an association management firm where she served as executive director for four of the 17 associations (two professional and two trade) managed by the company. From there she moved to the American Hospital Association and joined its Division of Personal Membership Groups as associate vice president, responsible for five of its professional societies. In 1995 she moved to New York to assume the helm of the Home Sewing Association.

Dave Fellers, CAE, has been executive director of the American Society of Plastic and Reconstructive Surgeons and the Plastic Surgery Educational Foundation in Arlington Heights, Ill., since 1991. Fellers is an ASAE Fellow, has been a CAE since 1978, and has been active in ASAE and the Association Forum. He has served as president of the Oklahoma and the Texas Societies of Association Executives. He is currently a member of the ASAE board of directors.

He has been involved in the American Association for Medical Society Executives (AAMSE) for the past six years. Currently a member of the board of directors, he also chaired the Online Task Force charged with implementing the AAMSE Web site, AAMSE Online. Fellers has served as chair of AAMSE's Organizational Effectiveness Task Force, which rewrote the evaluation criteria for the AAMSE evaluation program, and he has served as chair of the expansion of the AAMSE Membership Task Force.

Robin Kriegel, CAE, has been the executive director of the American Association of Medical Society Executives, a 1,200-member organization for medical society staff professionals, since January 1988. Prior to that, she spent 13 years at the National Student Nurses' Association in various positions, including director of membership services and director of organizational affairs. Her association management career began in 1972 at the National Association of Mens and Boys Apparel Clubs. Kriegel is an active member of the Chicago Society of Association Executives and the American Society of Association Executives. Inducted as an ASAE Fellow in 1990, she served as chair in 1996–97. She began a three-year term on the ASAE Foundation Board of Directors in July 1997.

Jeri A. Semer, CAE, is chief executive officer of ACUTA, an international professional association for college and university telecommunications managers with headquarters in Lexington, Ky. The association has 1,000 institutional and corporate members, a $1.4 million annual budget, and a staff of 10. Since joining the association in 1994, Semer has led her association through a major computer hardware and software upgrade, the development of a home page on the World Wide Web and electronic discussion groups, and development of policies/procedures for the management of electronic information services. Semer is a Fellow of the American Society of Association Executives and past president of the South Florida Association Executives. She currently serves on the boards of directors of the American Society of Association Executives and the Kentucky Society of Association Executives and is the 1997–98 chair of the ASAE Technology Section Council.

Bryan Silbermann, CAE, is president of the Produce Marketing Association (PMA), the largest, worldwide not-for-profit trade association representing companies that market fresh fruits, vegetables, flowers, and plants. PMA's membership of 2,500 ranges from supermarket retailers to farmers and foreign exporters to U.S. restaurant and hotel chains. The association's programs promote the sale and consumption of fresh produce and floral products worldwide. Since joining PMA in 1983, Silbermann's responsibilities have covered many aspects of research, training, government relations, information management, international trade, education, marketing, and public relations.

Ginger Nichols, CAE, has seen the association from all sides—as an association manager, board member, and now as a consultant to associations. From this experience, she has an intimate understanding of what makes an association successful in today's marketplace.

She began her association management career in 1974 with the American Society for Medical Technology, then temporarily left the association world for positions in communications and public affairs. In 1982, she moved to Washington, D.C., and accepted the post of director of communications and membership for the National Council of Community Mental Health Centers, where she spearheaded the association's first strategic planning initiative. After six successful years, Ginger accepted the challenge of establishing the first Membership Marketing Department at the National Business Forms Association. A major membership needs assessment that she implemented provided critical information for the association's strategic planning efforts and resulted in a record-setting recruitment campaign. After moving from Washington, D.C., to San Francisco in 1991, Nichols founded GinCommGroup to provide consulting and training in strategic planning, membership, marketing, and communications tailored to trade associations and professional societies.

ASAE Foundation

The Foundation's primary goal is to be the association community's essential and indispensable resource on the future. This goal is accomplished through environmental scanning, trend analysis, and funding innovative research that will create new knowledge and information for associations.

Mission

The ASAE Foundation, in cooperation with ASAE, is dedicated to enhancing the future effectiveness of the association community and to maximizing that community's impact on society through education and research.

You can support this work through your participation in the ASAE Foundation's annual giving campaign, sponsorship opportunities, and at various special events.

ASAE Publications

The American Society of Association Executives in Washington, DC, is an individual membership organization made up of more than 25,000 association executives and suppliers. Its members manage leading trade associations, individual membership societies, and voluntary organizations across the United States and in 44 countries around the globe. It also represents suppliers of products and services to the association community.

This book is one of the hundreds of titles available through the ASAE Bookstore. ASAE publications keep you a step ahead by providing you and your staff with valuable information resources for executive management, finance, human resources, membership, career management, fundraising, and technology.

A complete catalog of titles is available on the ASAE Web site at http://www.asaenet.org, or call the Member Service Center at 202/371-0940 for the latest printed catalog.